Consulting Authors

Michael A. DiSpezio
Global Educator
North Falmouth, Massachusetts

Marjorie Frank
*Science Writer and Content-Area Reading
    Specialist*
Brooklyn, New York

Michael Heithaus
Director, School of Environment and Society
*Associate Professor, Department of Biological
    Sciences*
Florida International University
North Miami, Florida

Donna Ogle
Professor of Reading and Language
National-Louis University
Chicago, Illinois

Program Advisors

Paul D. Asimow
*Professor of Geology and
    Geochemistry*
California Institute of Technology
Pasadena, California

Bobby Jeanpierre
*Associate Professor of Science
    Education*
University of Central Florida
Orlando, Florida

Gerald H. Krockover
*Professor of Earth and Atmospheric
    Science Education*
Purdue University
West Lafayette, Indiana

Rose Pringle
*Associate Professor
    School of Teaching and Learning*
College of Education
University of Florida
Gainesville, Florida

Carolyn Staudt
*Curriculum Designer for Technology
    KidSolve, Inc.*
The Concord Consortium
Concord, Massachusetts

Larry Stookey
Science Department
Antigo High School
Antigo, Wisconsin

Carol J. Valenta
*Senior Vice President and Associate
    Director of the Museum*
Saint Louis Science Center
St. Louis, Missouri

Barry A. Van Deman
President and CEO
Museum of Life and Science
Durham, North Carolina

iii

Power up with Science Fusion!

Your program fuses. . .

Online Virtual Experiences

Hands-on Explorations

Active Reading

. . .to generate science energy for you.

INDIANA
SCIENCE
FUSION

fusion [FYOO • zhuhn] a mixture or blend
formed by fusing two or more things

This Interactive Student Edition belongs to

_____

Teacher/Room

_____

 HOUGHTON MIFFLIN HARCOURT

HOUGHTON MIFFLIN HARCOURT

Front Cover: *lion cub* ©Cesar Lucas Abreu/Stone/Getty Images; *grass background* ©Nicholas Eveleigh/Stockbyte/ Getty Images; *field of tulips* ©John McAnulty/Corbis; *soccer players* ©Jon Feingersh Photography Inc/Blend Images/ Getty Images; *volcano* ©Westend61 GmbH/Alamy; *microscope* ©Thom Lang/Corbis.

Back Cover: *wind turbines* ©Comstock/Getty Images; *observatory* ©Robert Llewellyn/Workbook Stock/Getty Images; *giraffe* ©The Africa Image Library/Alamy; *guitar and saxophone* ©Brand Z/Alamy.

Active Reading

Be an active reader and make this book your own!

Write your ideas, answer questions, make notes, and record activity results right on these pages.

Your book will become a record of everything you learn in science.

Hands-on Explorations

Science is all about doing.

How Are Plants of the Same Kind Different?

Observe plants to compare and contrast them. How are plants of the same kind different?

Materials
bunch of carrots

① Observe the carrots to see how they are different. **Caution!** Do not eat the carrots.

② Draw and write your observations.

③ Compare your drawings. How can carrots be different from one another?

Do the exciting activities on the Inquiry Flipchart.

Ask questions and test your ideas.

Draw conclusions and share what you learn.

Online Virtual Experiences

Use a computer to make science come alive.

Explore cool labs and activities in the virtual world.

Science Fusion is new energy just for YOU!

Contents

PROCESS STANDARDS
Nature of Science

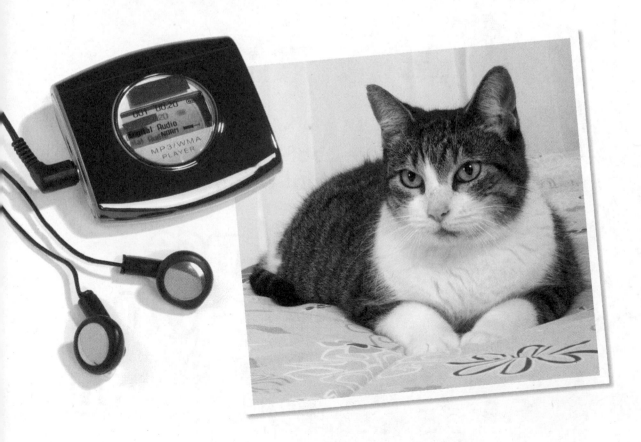

STANDARD 1
Physical Science

STANDARD 3
Life Science

STANDARD 4
Science, Engineering and Technology

PROCESS STANDARDS
Design Process

The Nature of Science

Children's Museum, Indianapolis, Indiana

I Wonder Why
Scientists study dinosaurs. Why?
Turn the page to find out.

Here's Why Scientists study dinosaurs to learn about animals that lived long ago.

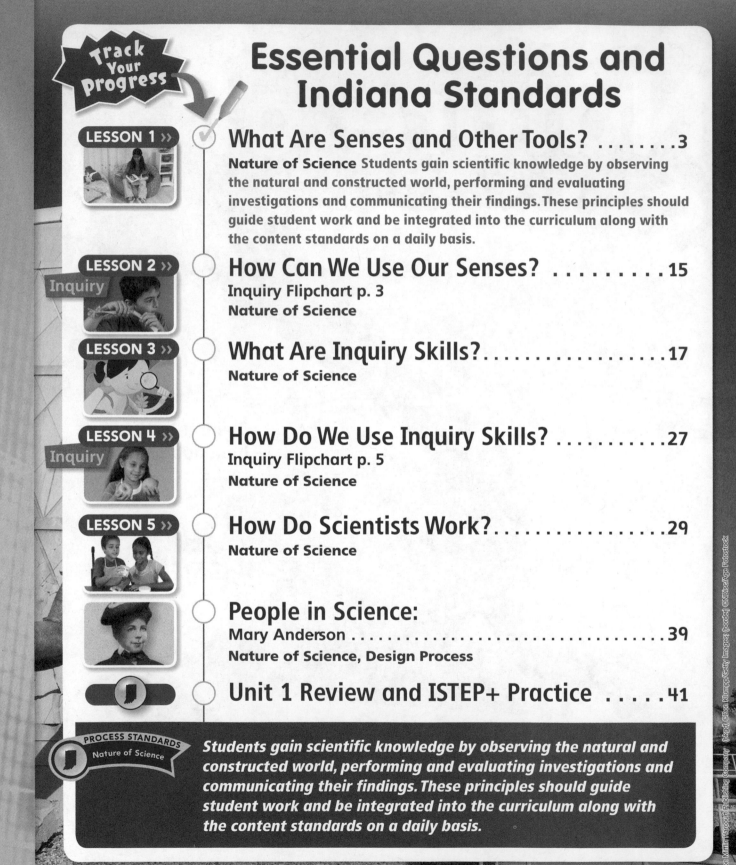

Track Your Progress

Essential Questions and Indiana Standards

PROCESS STANDARDS
Nature of Science

Students gain scientific knowledge by observing the natural and constructed world, performing and evaluating investigations and communicating their findings. These principles should guide student work and be integrated into the curriculum along with the content standards on a daily basis.

The Nature of Science Students gain scientific knowledge by observing the natural and constructed world, performing and evaluating investigations and communicating their findings. These principles should guide student work and be integrated into the curriculum along with the content standards on a daily basis.

Lesson **1**

Essential Question

What Are Senses and Other Tools?

🧠 Engage Your Brain!

Find the answer to the question in the lesson.

What sense is this child trying **not** to use?

the sense of

smell

Active Reading

Lesson Vocabulary

❶ Preview the lesson.

❷ Write the 2 vocabulary terms here.

_____   _____

Your Senses

How do you learn about things? You use your five senses. Your **senses** are the way you learn about the world. The senses are sight, hearing, smell, taste, and touch. You use different body parts for different senses.

Active Reading

The main idea is the most important idea about something. Draw two lines under the main idea.

You hear with your ears.

You smell with your nose.

You taste with your mouth.

You touch with your hands and skin.

You see with your eyes.

▶ Circle the name of the body parts you use for each sense.

5

Learning with Your Senses

How can your senses help you learn? Look at the pictures. What would your senses tell you about each thing?

Hearing
You listen to learn how things sound.

Touching
You touch to learn about texture—how things feel.

▶ **Underline how you learn how things feel.**

Seeing

You use sight to observe (color), (shape), and (size).

Smelling

You use smell to learn how things smell.

Tasting

You taste to learn if foods are sweet, sour, or salty.

▶ **You use sight to observe three things. Circle the words.**

Tools to Explore

You can use science tools to learn more. People use **science tools** to find out about things.

A hand lens is a science tool. It helps you see small things. You could not see these things as well with just your eyes.

Active Reading

Find the sentence that tells about **science tools**. Draw a line under the sentence.

These children are using a hand lens to closely observe a flower.

8

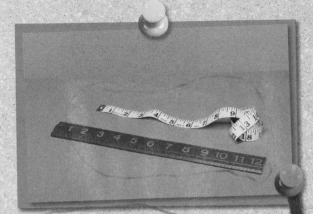

Ruler and Tape Measure

A ruler measures how long things are. A tape measure measures around things.

Measuring Cup

A measuring cup measures liquids.

Tools for Measuring

▶ Circle the names of tools you use to measure.

Balance

A balance compares how heavy things are.

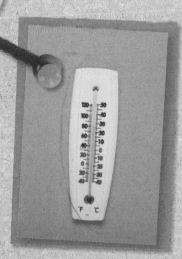

Thermometer

A thermometer measures temperature. It tells how hot and cold things are.

Measuring Up

Why should we use science tools to measure? What would happen if we used different things to measure the same object? We might get different measurements.

This girl is using her shoes to measure the rug.

Do the Math!

Measure Length

Measure how long a bookcase is. Use a small shoe, a large shoe, and a tape measure or a ruler. The tape measure or ruler measures in feet.

How long is the bookcase when you measure

1. with a small shoe?

   about _____ small shoes long

2. with a big shoe?

   about _____ big shoes long

3. with a ruler or tape measure?

   about _____ feet long

Why should you use a ruler or a tape measure to measure the bookcase?

_____

_____

_____

_____

Sum It Up!

1 Choose It!

Which tool is not used to measure? Mark an X on it.

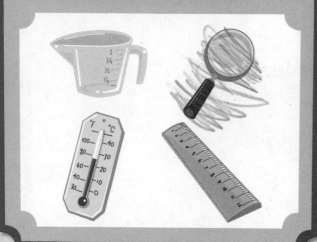

2 Circle It!

Which tool helps you observe small things? Circle it.

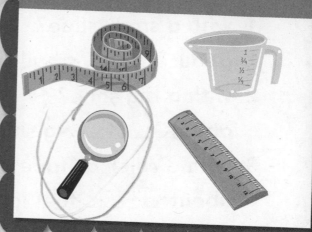

3 Match It!

Look at each thing. Which sense helps you learn about it? Draw lines to match them.

You touch to feel how furry something is.

You see to read.

You smell food baking.

Name _____

Word Play

You use different body parts for different senses. Label each body part with its sense.

| hearing | sight | smell | taste | touch |

Apply Concepts

Draw a line to the picture whose name completes the sentence.

❶ Measure a ball with a _____.

❷ Measure water with a _____.

❸ Observe an ant with a _____.

❹ Compare how heavy with a _____.

❺ Measure length with a _____.

**Take It Home!**

Family Members: Ask your child to tell how we use science tools and our senses to learn about the world. Play a game to name the senses or tools you use in different situations.

14

The Nature of Science Students gain scientific knowledge by observing the natural and constructed world, performing and evaluating investigations and communicating their findings. These principles should guide student work and be integrated into the curriculum along with the content standards on a daily basis.

Lesson 3

Essential Question

What Are Inquiry Skills?

Engage Your Brain!

Find the answer to the question in the lesson.

What can you infer this boy is doing?

The boy is

_____ .

Active Reading

Lesson Vocabulary

1 Preview the lesson.

2 Write the vocabulary term here.

_____

Skills to Help You Learn

Observe and Compare

How can you be like a scientist? You can use inquiry skills. **Inquiry skills** help you find out information. They help you learn about your world.

Active Reading

You can compare things. You find ways they are alike. A child on this page is comparing two things. Draw a triangle around the two things.

Falling Leaves Forest

observe

compare

18

Predict and Measure

I predict that it is going to rain today.

measure

predict

Rocky Cliff

▶ Circle the inquiry skill that helps you find the size of an object.

19

Classify and Communicate

classify

Bird Paradise

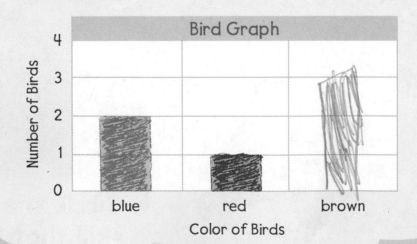

▶ **Complete the graph. How many brown birds are there?**

Bird Graph

Number of Birds — Color of Birds

blue   red   brown

communicate

Hypothesize and Plan an Investigation

A big log rolls farther than a small log because it is heavier.

I will roll both logs down the hill to test the hypothesis.

hypothesize

plan an investigation

Rolling Logs Hill

► Which child made a hypothesis? Draw a line under the hypothesis.

Infer and Draw Conclusions

I think the
light container
is empty.

Picnic
Palace

infer

Empty containers
are lighter than
full containers.

draw conclusions

▶ Underline the
conclusion the
child drew.

Make a Model and Sequence

▶ Things may happen in order.
Write 1 beside what happens first.
Write 2 beside what happens second.
Write 3 beside what happens third.
Write 4 beside what happens last.

Butterfly Garden

make a model

sequence

Sum It Up!

① Circle It!

You want to learn about something. Circle what you do to find out.

predict

classify

plan an investigation

② Choose It!

What inquiry skill does this show?

communicate

make a model

sequence

③ Draw It!

Observe an object. Draw it. Tell about it.

This is a _____. It is _____.

Brain Check

Name _____

Word Play

Circle the letters to spell the words.
Then complete the sentence.

compare	classify	infer	measure
observe	predict	sequence	

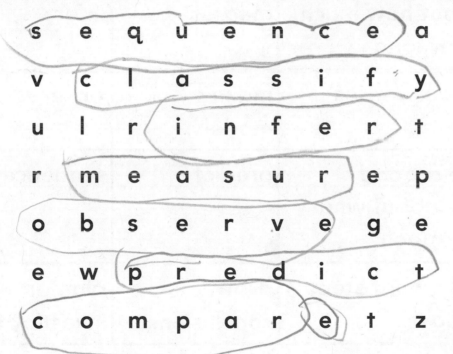

```
s e q u e n c e a
v c l a s s i f y
u l r i n f e r t
r m e a s u r e p
o b s e r v e g e
e w p r e d i c t
c o m p a r e t z
```

All the words in the puzzle
are _____ .

Apply Concepts

Circle the word that matches the meaning.

❶ tell what you learn	~~communicate~~ (circled)	observe
❷ sort things into groups	sequence	~~classify~~ (circled)
❸ tell how things are alike and different	make a model	~~compare~~ (circled)
❹ put things in order	~~sequence~~ (circled)	hypothesize
❺ find out how much or how long	~~measure~~ (circled)	infer
❻ use your senses	make a model	~~observe~~ (circled)
❼ make a good guess about what will happen	~~predict~~ (circled)	sequence
❽ decide what steps to follow	draw conclusions	~~plan an investigation~~ (circled)

Take It Home!

Family Members: Discuss with your child how inquiry skills are used around the home. For example, you measure when you cook and classify when you sort laundry.

Name _____

The Nature of Science Students gain scientific knowledge by observing the natural and constructed world, performing and evaluating investigations and communicating their findings. These principles should guide student work and be integrated into the curriculum along with the content standards on a daily basis.

Essential Question

How Do We Use Inquiry Skills?

Set a Purpose

Tell what you want to find out.

_____

_____

_____

Think About the Procedure

1 What fair test did you plan? Write your plan here.

_____

_____

2 What science tools will you use for your test?

_____

Record Your Data

Draw or write. Record what you observe.

Draw Conclusions

What conclusions can you draw?

_____

_____

Ask More Questions

What other questions could you ask?

_____

_____

Essential Question

How Do Scientists Work?

Engage Your Brain!

Find the answer to the question in the lesson.

How do you paint a rainbow using only three colors of paint?

You can mix

_____

Active Reading

Lesson Vocabulary

1 Preview the lesson.

2 Write the vocabulary term here.

_____

Think Like a Scientist

Scientists plan an investigation when they want to learn more. An **investigation** is a test scientists do. There are different plans for investigations. Here is one plan.

Observe

First, observe something. Ask a question about it.

Active Reading

Clue words can help you find the order of things. **First** is a clue word. Draw a box around this clue word.

What would happen if we mixed yellow paint and blue paint?

Hypothesize and Make a Plan

Next, make a hypothesis. State something you can test. Plan a fair test to see whether you are correct.

My Hypothesis

Blue paint and yellow paint mix to make green.

My Plan

1. Put yellow paint on a plate.
2. Put blue paint on a plate.
3. Mix the paints.

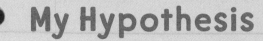

▶ Do you think yellow paint and blue paint mix to make green? Circle your answer.

Yes   No

Do the Test

Do the test. Follow the steps of your plan. Observe what happens.

We can mix the paints to see what happens.

Draw Conclusions

Draw conclusions from your test. What did you learn? Compare your results with your classmates' results. What would happen if you did the test again? How do you know?

If we do the test again, yellow paint and blue paint will still make green.

▶ Circle the color that yellow and blue make when you mix them.

Record What You Observe

Scientists record what they learn from an investigation. You can keep a record in a science notebook. You can draw pictures. You can write.

Active Reading

A detail is a fact about a main idea. Draw one line under a detail. Draw an arrow to the main idea it tells about.

▶ **What colors make green?**

_____

Sum It Up!

① Write It!

You have a ✦ and a ▪.
You will drop them.
You think the block will fall faster.
How can you test your idea?

_____

② Circle It!

You do the steps in an investigation.
Now you draw what happens.
Which step are you doing?
Circle it.

Observe.   Plan a fair test.

Record what you observe.

Name _____

Word Play

Unscramble the word to complete each sentence. Use these words if you need help.

| observe | hypothesize | investigation | record |

ntiovetigansi

1 To learn more about something, you do an _____.

eyhtpoheszi

2 When you make a statement you can test, you _____.

dreorc

3 After you do a test, you should _____ your results.

beosver

4 When you look at something closely, you _____ it.

Apply Concepts

Can air move a penny and a feather?
Tell how you could investigate.
Write a number from 1 to 5 to show the order.

———————— Write a plan.

———————— Ask a question–
Can air move a penny and a feather?

———————— Record what you observe.

———————— Share your results.

———————— Follow your plan.

Family Members: Ask your child to tell you about the steps of an investigation. Then plan an investigation you and your child can try at home.

People in Science

Learn About...
Mary Anderson

In 1902, Mary Anderson observed something. In bad weather, drivers had trouble seeing. They had to drive with the window open. Or they had to get out to clean off the windshield. Anderson got an idea. She invented the windshield wiper.

Drivers could use it from inside their vehicle. They could see the road and stay warm and dry.

Fun Fact

By the 1920s all cars had windshield wipers.

39

This Leads to That

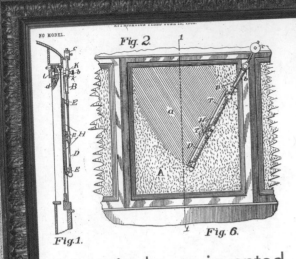

Mary Anderson invented the first windshield wiper. This shows an early drawing.

Robert Kearns invented a windshield wiper that went on and off as needed.

▶ **How does Mary Anderson's invention help people today?**

_____

_____

_____

Name _____

Multiple Choice

Fill in the circle next to the best answer.

Nature of Science

1 What can these children learn from listening to the music?

- ○ how it feels
- ○ how it looks
- ○ how it sounds

Nature of Science

2 You observe the plants. You think about what you know. You use these things to decide what something means. What are you doing?

LIGHT AND WARM   DARK AND WARM

- ○ classifying the plants
- ○ drawing a conclusion
- ○ predicting what will happen

Nature of Science

3 What step in a scientific method is shown here?

- ○ comparing results
- ○ doing a test
- ○ observing

Nature of Science

4 Which sentence compares the lemon and the banana?

- ○ The banana has a soft inside.
- ○ The lemon is very sour.
- ○ Both fruits are yellow.

Nature of Science

5 You investigate to find out whether clay or sand holds more water. What can you do to record what you observe?

- ○ draw a picture
- ○ tell a friend
- ○ think about it

Nature of Science

6 How do you know an apple is larger than a grape?

- ○ You measure them.
- ○ You sort them.
- ○ You taste them.

Nature of Science

7 Which sense is this boy using to observe the flower?

○ hearing
○ smell
○ taste

Nature of Science

8 You are reading a book. Which sense are you using?

○ sight
○ smell
○ taste

Nature of Science

9 You want to find out whether an apple tastes sweeter than a peach. Which will you use?

○ your eyes
○ your hands
○ your mouth

Nature of Science

10 What can you observe with a hand lens?

○ how a small object looks
○ how a small object smells
○ how much a small object weighs

Nature of Science

11 You want to measure a rock's length. Which science tool will you use?

○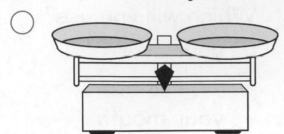

○

○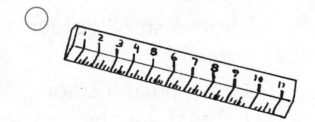

Nature of Science

12 How are these tools the SAME?

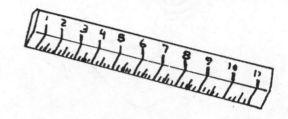

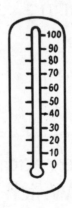

○ You can use them to find direction.

○ You can use them to measure.

○ You can use them to observe the parts of small things.

Nature of Science

13 When do you make a hypothesis?

○ after an investigation

○ as you are doing an investigation

○ before testing an idea

Nature of Science

14 You want to find out how this ride works. Why would making a model be helpful?

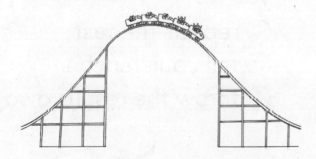

○ It would be the same size as a real ride.

○ It would work in a way that was similar to a real ride.

○ You would not have to observe.

Nature of Science

15 You tell what happens first, next, and last in an activity. Which inquiry skill is this?

○ hypothesize

○ infer

○ sequence

Nature of Science

16 You want to find out which car rolls the longer distance. What question do you ask?

○ Which car is older?

○ Which car will roll farther?

○ Why do cars roll?

Nature of Science

17 What step in a scientific method is shown?

○ doing a test
○ drawing a conclusion
○ recording results

Nature of Science

18 You want to compare the hardness of two objects. You run a fair test. How do you set up the test?

○ You test only one object.
○ You test both objects the same way.
○ You test one object one way and the other object a different way.

Nature of Science

19 How could you record what you learn from an investigation?

○ do a test
○ draw a picture
○ make a plan

Nature of Science

20 You and a classmate compare your results. The results are not the same. What should you do?

○ repeat the test
○ tell your teacher
○ throw the results away

All About Materials

Lighthouse,
Michigan City, Indiana

I Wonder Why

People used different materials to build this lighthouse. Why?
Turn the page to find out.

Here's Why The lighthouse is made of glass, brick, and metal. These materials have to fit the job they do.

Track Your Progress

Essential Questions and Indiana Standards

STANDARD 1
Physical Science

Describe objects in terms of the materials that compose them and their physical properties.

Essential Question

What Materials Make Up Objects?

Engage Your Brain!

Find the answer to the question in the lesson.

What could you make with this wood?

_____

Active Reading

Lesson Vocabulary

1 Preview the lesson.

2 Write the 3 vocabulary terms here.

_____ _____

_____ _____

Play Your Part

Objects may be made of different parts. The parts go together to make the whole.

Look at this bicycle. It has wheels, a frame, and other parts. These parts go together to make a bicycle.

Active Reading

A detail is a fact about a main idea. Draw a line under a detail. Draw an arrow to the main idea it tells about.

seat

wheel

pedal

▶ Write labels for the parts of the bicycle.

Baskit

fha flp

bicycle

51

A Material World

Look at this house. One part is brick. Another part is metal. Other parts are wood. The windows are glass.

Brick, metal, wood, and glass are materials. **Materials** are what objects are made of.

Active Reading

Find the sentence that tells the meaning of **materials**. Draw a line under the sentence.

brick

wood

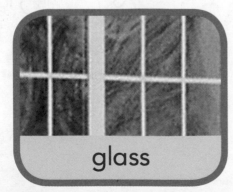

glass

metal

► Write labels to name four materials in this house.

53

Made to Order

Materials are natural or human-made. **Natural** materials are found in nature. For example, cotton is from a plant. Wood is from trees.

People make **human-made** materials such as plastics and nylon. Scientists first made them in a lab. Scientists changed petroleum into these new materials not found in nature.

trees

cotton

Crude Oil

petroleum

cotton shirt

wooden boat with nylon sail

Some objects are made of natural materials. Others are made of human-made materials. Some objects are made of both natural and human-made materials.

▶ **Mark an X on the object made from both natural and human-made materials.**

plastic toys

Everyday Materials

Do you have a pair of jeans? Cotton jeans are made in factories. Here is how.

Active Reading

Things may happen in order. Draw a line under the step that happens first.

1

Looms weave cotton into cloth.

2

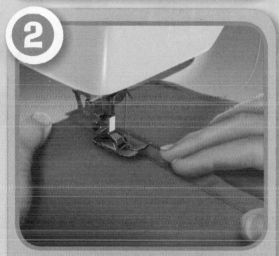

Workers use machines to cut and sew the cloth.

3

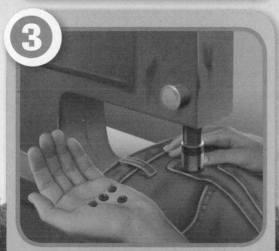

Workers use machines to put on metal rivets.

4 Now the jeans are ready to wear!

Sum It Up!

① Draw It!

Draw something made of glass on the house.

② Match It!

Draw a line to match each toy with the kind of material it is made from.

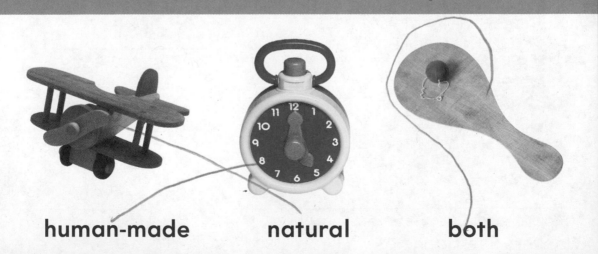

human-made   natural   both

Name _____

Word Play

Color the letters to spell the vocabulary words. Write the words to complete the sentences.

| human-made | materials | natural |

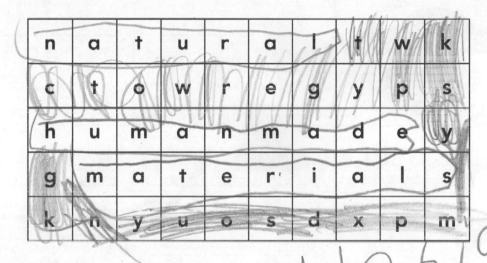

n	a	t	u	r	a	l	t	w	k
c	t	o	w	r	e	g	y	p	s
h	u	m	a	n	m	a	d	e	y
g	m	a	t	e	r	i	a	l	s
k	n	y	u	o	s	d	x	p	m

❶ Objects are made of _materials_.

❷ Materials made in a lab are _humanmade_.

❸ Materials found in nature are _natural_.

Apply Concepts

Complete the chart. Name and classify the materials each object is made from.

Materials Chart

Object	Material	Natural, human-made, or both
1 	_____ _____	_____
2	_____ _____	_____
3	_____ _____	_____

 **Family Members:** Play a game with your child to identify the parts and materials of objects around the home. Classify the materials as natural, human-made, or both.

Take It Home!

Name _____

Essential Question

What Can We Observe About Objects?

1.1.1 Use all senses as appropriate to identify the component parts of objects and the materials from which they are made.

Set a Purpose

Tell what you want to find out.

_____

_____

Think About the Procedure

❶ What senses will you use to observe?

_____

_____

❷ How will you tell what the parts and materials are?

_____

_____

Record Your Data

Record what you observe about your object.

Sense	Observation
Touch	
Hearing	
Sight	

Draw Conclusions

Draw your object. Label each part. Name the material that makes up each part.

Ask More Questions

What other questions could you ask about the parts and materials that make up objects?

_____

_____

1.4.1 Use all senses as appropriate to sort objects as being composed of materials that are naturally-occurring or human-made, or a combination of the two.

Name _____

Essential Question

How Can Materials Be Sorted?

Set a Purpose

Tell what you want to do.

_____

Think About the Procedure

❶ What will you observe about the objects?

_____

_____

❷ How will you sort the objects?

_____

_____

Record Your Data

Draw or write to show how you sorted the objects.

Natural	Human-made	Both

Draw Conclusions

How could you tell what objects were made of?

_____

_____

Ask More Questions

What other questions could you ask about objects and materials?

_____

_____

Ask a Polymer Scientist

What are polymers?

Polymers are a kind of material. We can find some polymers, such as silk, in nature. Scientists make other polymers, such as plastics.

What does a polymer scientist do?

I work with different materials to make them better. Materials can cause problems. I try to solve the problems.

What is one problem that polymer scientists are working on?

Some polymers take years to break down. This makes a lot of garbage. Scientists want to make polymers that break down faster so there is less garbage.

Now It's Your Turn!

▶ **What question would you ask?**

_____

_____

_____

_____

Polymer Play

▶ **Think about what a polymer scientist studies. Make a list of polymers on the lines below.**

rubber ball

foam peanuts

plastic toy

1 _____

2 _____

3 _____

4 _____

plastic bags

 **Fun Fact**

A lobster's shell is a polymer.

Essential Question

What Are Solids, Liquids, and Gases?

Engage Your Brain!

Find the answer to the question in the lesson.

How is water different from stone and metal?

_____

Active Reading

Lesson Vocabulary

1 Preview the lesson.

2 Write the 5 vocabulary terms here.

_____ _____

_____ _____

_____

It All Matters

How are towels, water, and balloons the same? They are all matter.

Matter is anything that takes up space. It has mass. **Mass** is the amount of matter something has.

Matter may be different. Different kinds of matter are solids, liquids, and gases.

Active Reading

Clue words can help you find ways things are the same. Draw a box around the clue word **same**.

> ► Circle three things in this picture that are made of matter.

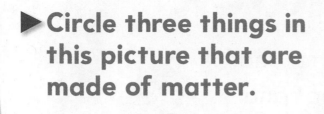

Do the Math!

Order by Mass

You can measure mass with a balance.

► Order the objects by mass. Write 1 for least mass. Write 3 for most mass.

book

marker

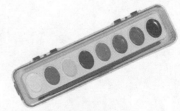

paint

_____ _____ _____

Solid as a Rock

A **solid** is a kind of matter that keeps its shape. The flip-flops and towels are solids. What happens if you move a flip-flop? It still keeps its shape.

What other solids could you find at a pool party?

flip-flops

towels

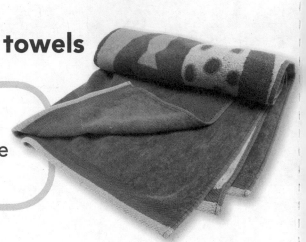

juice

Lovely Liquid

A **liquid** is matter that flows. It takes the shape of its container. Look at the juice. It pours from the pitcher to the glass. It takes the shape of each container.

What a Gas!

A **gas** is the only kind of matter that fills all of the space in its container. It does not have its own shape. The gas in the balloons spreads to fill all the space.

bubbles

balloons

▶ **What kind of matter is inside the bubbles?**

_____

A Matter of Fact

▶ Write <u>yes</u> or <u>no</u> in the first four columns. In the last column, write <u>solid</u> or <u>liquid</u> to classify each one.

Are These Objects Solids or Liquids?

	Does it have mass?	Does it take up space?
lemonade	yes	yes
sunglasses		
dish soap		

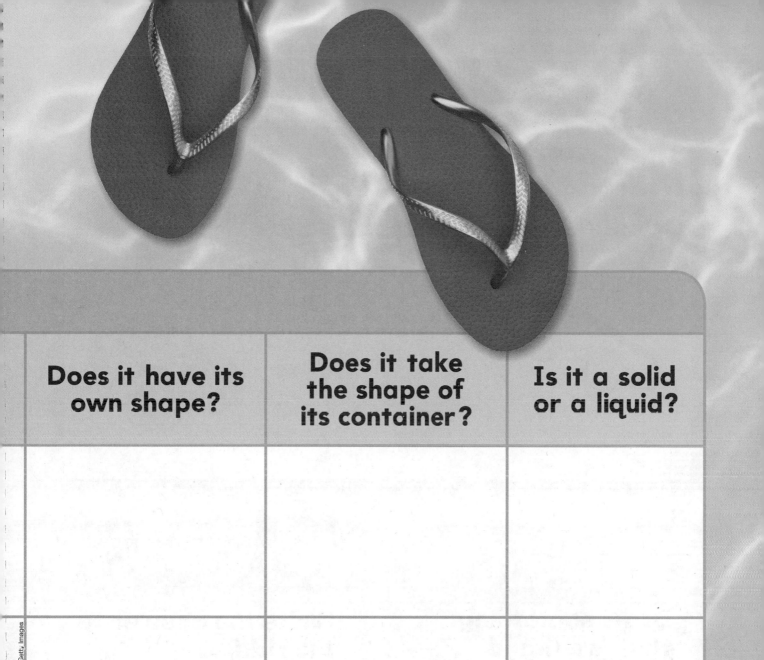

Does it have its own shape?	Does it take the shape of its container?	Is it a solid or a liquid?

Sum It Up!

① Circle It!

Circle the objects that are solids.

② Draw It!

Draw something that is a liquid.

③ Write It!

Write the answer to the riddle.

I am a kind of matter you might know.

I spread out and seem to grow.

I have mass and take up space.

Put me in a case and I fill the case.

What am I? _____

Brain Check

Name _____

Word Play

Color each solid **red**. Color each liquid **blue**.
Color each gas **yellow**.

Apply Concepts

Write to complete the chart.

Solids, Liquids, and Gases

Kind of Matter	Definition
solid	• _____ _____
_____	• flows • takes the shape of its container
_____	• fills all the space in its container

Write to complete the sentence.

All matter has _____

and takes up _____.

1.1.2 Characterize materials as solid or liquid, investigate their properties, record observations and explain the choices to others based on evidence (e.g. physical properties).

Name _____

Essential Question

How Can We Classify Matter?

Set a Purpose

Tell what you want to find out.

_____

Think About the Procedure

1 What will you do with the beans and then the water?

_____

_____

2 How will you know whether beans and water are liquid or solid?

_____

_____

Record Your Data

Draw to show beans and water in each container.

	Beans	Water
Container 1		
Container 2		
Container 3		

Draw Conclusions

Are beans solid or liquid? Is water solid or liquid?
Tell how you know.

_____

_____

_____

Ask More Questions

What questions could you ask about classifying matter?

_____

_____

Inquiry Flipchart p. 12

Lesson

INQUIRY **6**

1.1.3 Predict the results of, and experiment with methods (e.g., sieving, evaporation) for separating solids and liquids based on their physical properties.

Name _____

Essential Question

How Can We Separate Solids and Liquids?

Set a Purpose

Tell what you want to do.

_____

Think About the Procedure

❶ What do you think will happen when you pour the mixture through the sieve?

_____

_____

❷ What do you think will happen when you put the mixture in a warm place?

_____

_____

Record Your Data

Draw or write to show what happened to the mixture.

sieve	
warm place	

Draw Conclusions

How did you separate the beans and the salt from the water?

_____

_____

_____

Ask More Questions

What other questions could you ask about separating solids and liquids?

_____

_____

Review and ISTEP+ Practice

Name _____

Multiple Choice

Fill in the circle next to the best answer.

1.1.1

1 Which is TRUE about materials?

○ All materials are human-made.

○ Materials are used to make objects.

○ Human-made materials are found in nature.

1.1.1

2 This window has a wood frame and a glass pane.

What materials make up the window?

○ plastic

○ wood only

○ wood and glass

1.1.1

❸ Which are parts of the boy's skates?

○ a helmet and
  elbow pads
○ knee pads
○ wheels

1.4.1

❹ Where do natural materials come from?

○ They are found
  in nature.
○ They are made
  in factories.
○ People make them.

1.1.1

❺ Cara is playing with two toys. Which toy is made from paper?

○ both toys
○ only the airplane
○ only the bucket

Use this picture to answer questions 6–8.

1.1.1

6 What are the guitar's body, strings, and keys?
○ music from the guitar
○ parts of the guitar
○ tools of the guitar

1.4.1

7 The body of this guitar is made from wood. Which kind of material is wood?
○ both human-made and natural
○ only human-made
○ only natural

1.4.1

8 The strings of this guitar are made from nylon. Which kind of material is nylon?
○ both human-made and natural
○ only human-made
○ only natural

1.4.1

9 Which object is made from natural materials?
○ a nylon shirt
○ a plastic bottle
○ a wood table

1.4.1

10 Where did human-made materials first come from?
○ They were made in a lab.
○ They were found in space.
○ They were found in nature.

© Houghton Mifflin Harcourt Publishing Company (border) ©NDisc/Age Fotostock

1.1.2

11 What is mass?

○ what everything is made of

○ the temperature of an object

○ the amount of matter something has

1.1.2

12 Which tool can you use to measure mass?

○ a balance

○ a ruler

○ a thermometer

1.1.2

13 How is all matter the SAME?

○ All matter is solid.

○ All matter takes up space.

○ All matter is made from natural materials.

1.1.2

14 Which object is solid?

○ the boat

○ the ocean

○ the wind

1.1.2

15 Which kind of matter flows?

○ gas
○ liquid
○ solid

1.1.2

16 Which kind of matter keeps its own shape?

○ gas
○ liquid
○ solid

1.1.3

17 You put sand in a glass of water. Then you put the glass of water in a sunny window. What will you observe after a few weeks?

○ The glass will have only water.
○ The glass will have only sand.
○ The glass will be empty.

1.1.3

18 You want to separate a mixture of a solid and a liquid. What tool can you use?

○ a balance
○ a sieve
○ a thermometer

Use this picture to answer questions 19 and 20.

1.1.3

19 Mrs. May is using a sieve. What will flow out of the sieve?

○ rocks

○ shells

○ water

1.1.3

20 Mrs. May wants to find shells. How can she use the sieve to find shells?

○ She can use it to separate shells from rocks.

○ She can use it to hold water.

○ She can use it to separate shells from water.

White River Gardens,
Indianapolis, Indiana

I Wonder Why

Plants grow well in the soil at this garden. Why?
Turn the page to find out.

Here's Why The soil at this garden is rich, or good for growing plants. Rich soil has many bits of once-living things.

Track Your Progress

Essential Questions and Indiana Standards

STANDARD 2
Earth and Space Science

Observe, describe, and ask questions about soil components and properties.

1.2.1 Observe and compare properties of sand, clay, silt and organic matter. Look for evidence of sand, clay, silt and organic matter as components of soil samples. **1.2.3** Observe a variety of soil samples and describe in words and pictures the soil properties in terms of color, particle size and shape, texture, and recognizable living and nonliving items in the soil.

Essential Question

What Is Soil?

Engage Your Brain!

Find the answer to the question in the lesson.

How can people use soil?

to _____

Active Reading

Lesson Vocabulary

1 Preview the lesson.

2 Write the 5 vocabulary terms here.

_____   _____

_____   _____

_____

Super Soil

Soil is made up of small pieces of rock and once-living things. We use soil to grow plants.

Active Reading

Find the sentence that tells the meaning of **soil**. Draw a line under the sentence.

Soil forms a layer on parts of Earth's surface.

Soil forms when wind and water break down rock. The bits of rock form the base of soil.

At the same time, dead plants and animals fall to the ground. These once-living things break down into bits. The bits become part of soil, too.

Soil is a mix of many tiny pieces.

▶ **What can you observe about this soil?** _____

_____

The Scoop on Soil

Sand, silt, clay, and once-living things make up soil. Different amounts of these parts make soils different.

Active Reading

Find the sentence that tells what **sand** is made of. Draw a line under the sentence.

Garden soil has many once-living things.

Soil is a mix of these four parts.

Sand is made of large bits of rock. It does not hold water well.

Silt is made of medium bits of rock. It holds water fairly well.

Clay is made of small bits of rock. Clay holds water so well that clay sticks together.

Once-living things are bits of dead plants and animals. They make soil rich, or good for plants.

▶ **Circle the part of soil that makes soil good for growing plants.**

In the Mix

There are many soils. But each soil is a mix of things. The mix gives each soil different properties. A **property** is one part of what something is like. The chart on the right shows some properties of soil.

Active Reading

Clue words can help you find ways things are different. **But** and **different** are clue words. Draw boxes around these words.

This rich garden soil is dark brown.

▶ Write labels to complete the chart.

Color The rock in soil helps give soil its color. Soil can be orange, gray, tan, and yellow, too.

red ___*tan*___ black

Size of Rock Bits The rock bits may be different sizes. Clay has small bits. Sand has large ones.

  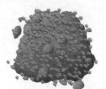

small medium ___*large*___

Texture The size and shape of the rock bits make soils feel different.

___*smooth*___ gritty lumpy

Amount of Once-Living Things Once-living things make soil rich. Rich soil is good for plants.

 dung

few ___*some*___ many

95

Sum It Up!

① Write It!

List the four parts that make up soil.

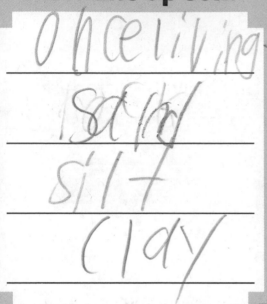

once living things
sand
silt
clay

② Order It!

Write 1, 2, 3 to order how a plant becomes part of soil.

2 The plant begins to break into pieces.

1 A plant dies and falls to the ground.

3 The pieces get smaller and become part of soil.

③ Draw It!

Draw soil that has these properties.

tan   large rock bits   gritty   few once-living things

Dig it!

Name _____

Word Play

Match each part of soil to its description.
Then add another property it has.

sand

It holds water so well that it sticks together.

_____

_____

silt

It does not hold water well.

_____

_____

clay

It is made of medium bits of rock.

_____

_____

Apply Concepts

Fill in the chart. Show how soil forms.

How Soil Forms

```
┌─────────────────────────────────────┐
│                                     │
│                                     │
│                                     │
│                                     │
│                                     │
│                                     │
└─────────────────────────────────────┘
                  │
                  ▼
┌─────────────────────────────────────┐
│                                     │
│                                     │
│                                     │
│                                     │
│                                     │
│                                     │
└─────────────────────────────────────┘
                  │
                  ▼
┌─────────────────────────────────────┐
│   All the bits mix together to      │
│          make soil.                 │
└─────────────────────────────────────┘
```

Take It Home!

Family Members: Walk with your child near your home to observe soil. Have your child name some properties of the soil.

1.2.1 Observe and compare properties of sand, clay, silt and organic matter. Look for evidence of sand, clay, silt and organic matter as components of soil samples.
1.2.2 Choose, test, and use tools to separate soil samples into component parts.

Name _____

Essential Question

What Do We Find in Soil?

Set a Purpose

Tell what you want to find out.

_____

_____

Think About the Procedure

❶ What tools do you have?

_____

❷ Tell about one way you will use a tool to separate the soil into parts.

_____

_____

Record Your Data

Draw and label the parts in your soil sample.

Draw Conclusions

What parts make up your soil?

_____

_____

Ask More Questions

What other questions can you ask about soil?

_____

_____

100

Name _____

1.2.1 Observe and compare properties of sand, clay, silt and organic matter. Look for evidence of sand, clay, silt and organic matter as components of soil samples.
1.2.3 Observe a variety of soil samples and describe in words and pictures the soil properties in terms of color, particle size and shape, texture, and recognizable living and nonliving items in the soil.

Essential Question

How Do Soils Differ?

Set a Purpose

Tell what you want to find out.

_____

Think About the Procedure

❶ How many soil samples will you compare?

_____

❷ Name some properties of soil that you will observe.

_____

_____

_____

Record Your Data

Draw and write to record what you observe.

Property	Soil Sample 1	Soil Sample 2
Color		
Texture		
Size and Shape of Bits		
Living or Once-living Things		

Draw Conclusions

How are the soils the same? How are they different?

_____

_____

_____

Ask More Questions

What other questions could you ask about soil?

_____

_____

102

1.2.4 Observe over time the effect of organisms such as earthworms in the formation of soil from dead plants. Discuss the importance of earthworms in soil.

Essential Question

How Do Earthworms Help Soil?

Engage Your Brain!

Find the answer to the question in the lesson.

What do earthworms eat that helps plants?

They eat _dirt_.

Active Reading

Lesson Vocabulary

1. Preview the lesson.
2. Write the 2 vocabulary terms here.

earth worms   compost

The Worms Crawl In

Soil is rich when earthworms are at work. An **earthworm** is a small animal. Earthworms live in soil. They eat the soil and tunnel in the soil. Both these things help make soil better for plants to grow in.

Active Reading

An effect tells what happens. Draw two lines under an effect of what earthworms do.

Earthworm tunnels hold water. They also give plant roots more space to grow.

© Houghton Mifflin Harcourt Publishing Company • © Oceana/Photo Researchers, Inc.

Earthworm waste helps plants grow.

Earthworms move soil. This adds air to soil. It also helps break down once-living things.

Do the Math!
Measure Earthworms

Use a 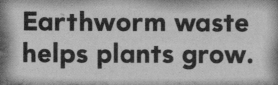 to measure each earthworm. Circle the longest one.

Compost It!

Compost is a material made up of bits of dead plants. Compost makes soil rich. It cuts down on garbage, too.

People make compost at home. They put kitchen and yard waste in a bin. They may add water and earthworms.

Active Reading

Things may happen in order. Write **1** beside what happens first.

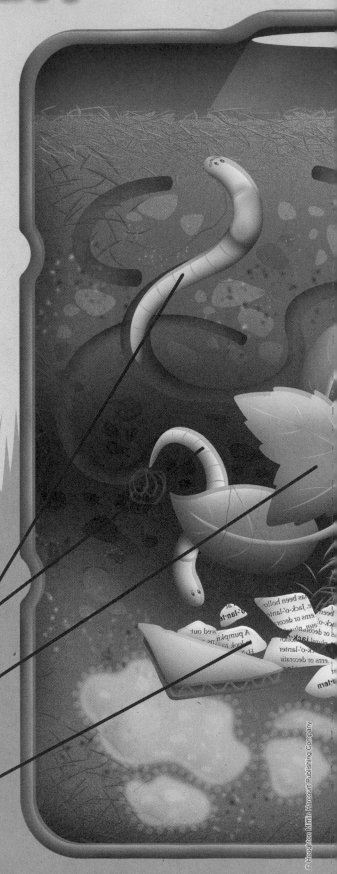

worms

leaves

paper

Over time, the waste breaks down. The worms help it break down faster. The material that is left is compost.

▶ **Circle the worms.**

wood chips

kitchen waste

water

grass

air

Sum It Up!

① Solve It!

Write the answer to this riddle.

My life is all about soil.

I live in soil.

I eat soil.

I make soil better for plants to grow.

What am I?

worm's

② Write It!

Write one way earthworms help make soil rich.

they poup out it

?

?

③ Choose It!

Circle the thing that can go in a compost bin.

 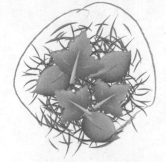 

Name _____

Word Play

Write words from the box to label the photo.

| earthworms | tunnel | plant roots |

_____

_____

_____

Apply Concepts

Fill in the chart to tell a cause or an effect.

Cause	Effect
Earthworms eat soil and make waste.	_____ _____ _____
_____ _____ _____	This helps break down once-living things.
Earthworms tunnel in soil.	_____ _____ _____
Compost is made up of bits of dead plants.	_____ _____ _____

Take It Home!

Family Members: You can often see earthworms after a heavy rain. Observe them with your child. What do earthworms look like? What do they do?

1.2.3 Observe a variety of soil samples and describe in words and pictures the soil properties in terms of color, particle size and shape, texture, and recognizable living and nonliving items in the soil; **Nature of Science**

People in Science

Learn About...
Dr. George Washington Carver

Dr. George Washington Carver was a scientist. He worked with farmers. Dr. Carver showed them how to plant peanuts to keep their soil good for growing crops.

Fun Fact

Dr. Carver invented peanut shampoo!

This Leads to That

Dr. George Washington Carver studied farming.

He taught farmers how to make their soil rich.

Today, farmers around the world use his ideas.

▶ **How did Dr. Carver help farmers?**

_____

_____

_____

Multiple Choice

Fill in the circle next to the best answer.

1.2.1

1 What makes up soil?

○ only once-living things

○ only rocks and water

○ once-living things and rocks

1.2.3

2 Nick knows that soils with different textures are made of different materials. How does he know?

○ He places the soils in boxes.

○ He observes the soils carefully.

○ He plants a shrub in one of the soils.

Nature of Science

3 What can this bag of soil be used for?

Soil

○ feeding animals

○ growing plants

○ making rocks

1.2.3

❹ Jill wants to observe the size of the bits in this soil. Which tool should she use?

○ a balance
○ a hand lens
○ a thermometer

1.2.1

❺ Which does not hold water well?
○ clay
○ sand
○ silt

1.2.1, 1.2.3

❻ Why are soils different colors?
○ They get different amounts of rain.
○ They have different materials in them.
○ They hold different amounts of water.

1.2.1

❼ What is silt made of?
○ large bits of rock
○ medium bits of rock
○ small bits of rock

1.2.1

8 The soil around Rico's house is mostly sand. What can Rico add to his garden to grow plants better?

○ clay

○ once-living things

○ rocks

1.2.1

9 Which is made of the smallest bits of rock?

○ clay

○ sand

○ silt

1.2.1

10 How do plants become part of soil?

○ Wind and rain break them down.

○ They die and break down into tiny bits.

○ They turn into rocks.

1.2.4

11 Many earthworms are in your garden. What does this tell you about the soil in your garden?

○ It has a lot of clay in it.

○ It has many rocks.

○ It is good soil for growing plants.

1.2.4

12 How do earthworm tunnels make soil better?

○ They add rocks to soil.

○ They break down once-living things.

○ They hold water and give roots more space to grow.

1.2.4

13 Why do people add earthworms to a compost bin?

○ Earthworms cut down on garbage.

○ Earthworms help waste break down faster.

○ Earthworms help waste break down more slowly.

1.2.2

14 Tim is using tools to separate soil into parts. Which tool could he use?

○ a balance

○ a sieve

○ a thermometer

Use this information to answer questions 15–18.

Aisha uses a hand lens to observe these bits from three different soils.

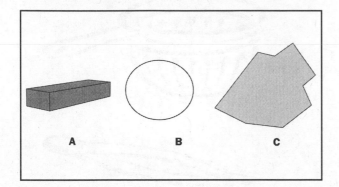

A   B   C

1.2.3

15 What is one property that Aisha can compare?
- ○ shape
- ○ hardness
- ○ amount of once-living things

1.2.3

16 Which soil has the LARGEST bits?
- ○ soil A
- ○ soil B
- ○ soil C

1.2.3

17 What is TRUE about soil B?
- ○ It has the lightest color of the soils.
- ○ It has the roughest texture of the soils.
- ○ It holds the most water of the soils.

1.2.1, 1.2.3

18 Soil with a lot of sand has large rough bits. Which is MOST LIKELY sandy soil?
- ○ soil A
- ○ soil B
- ○ soil C

1.2.2

19 Why would a scientist separate soil into its parts?

○ to find out its color

○ to find out its texture

○ to find out what parts make it up

1.2.2

20 Which tool would be BEST for separating large rocks from soil?

○

○

○

Living Things

STANDARD 3
Life Science

The cardinal is Indiana's state bird.

I Wonder Why

A female cardinal is tan. Why?

Turn the page to find out.

Here's Why Her tan color helps the female cardinal hide when she cares for her chicks.

Track Your Progress

Essential Questions and Indiana Standards

STANDARD 3 Life Science

Observe, describe and ask questions about living things and their relationship to their environment.

1.3.2 Observe organisms closely over a period of time in different habitats, such as terrariums, aquariums, lawns, and trees. Draw and write about observations. **1.3.3** Observe and explain that plants and animals have basic needs for growth and survival: plants need to take in water and need light and animals need to take in water and food and have a way to dispose of waste.

Lesson **1**

Essential Question

What Are Some Kinds of Living Things?

Engage Your Brain!

Find the answer to the question in the lesson.

How is this plant like some animals?

_____

_____

Active Reading

Lesson Vocabulary

1 Preview the lesson.

2 Write the 2 vocabulary terms here.

_____   _____

Living It Up!

Living things are people, animals, and plants. They need food, water, air, and space to live. Living things also need ways to get rid of waste.

flowers

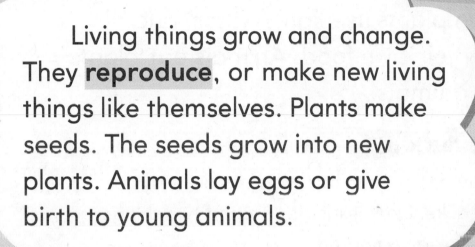

Living things grow and change. They **reproduce**, or make new living things like themselves. Plants make seeds. The seeds grow into new plants. Animals lay eggs or give birth to young animals.

▶ **Label the living things you see in the picture.**

Plant or Animal?

Plants and animals are both living things. But plants and animals are different, too. Plants stay in one place. Animals can move on their own.

Green plants use light, water, and air to make their own food. Animals eat plants or other animals.

Active Reading

When you compare things, you find out ways they are alike. Draw triangles around two things that are being compared.

124

▶ Complete the chart to tell how plants and animals are different.

	Plants	Animals
make their own food	Yes	no
eat plants or animals	no	Yes
move around on their own	no	Yes
grow and change	Yes	Yes

A Venus flytrap is different from most other plants. It moves its leaves to catch insects and spiders. Then it eats what it catches.

Sum It Up!

① Circle It!

Circle each living thing.

② Solve It!

Solve the riddle.

Some living things fly.
Some walk, run,
    or swim.
I do not move on
    my own.
I stay in one place.

What am I?

Plant

③ Choose It!

Circle each group of words that tells about an animal.

eats plants or animals

makes its own food

grows and changes

moves around on its own

1.3.2 Observe organisms closely over a period of time in different habitats, such as terrariums, aquariums, lawns, and trees. Draw and write about observations.

Name _____

Essential Question

What Can We Observe About Living Things?

Set a Purpose
Tell what you want to find out.

_____

_____

Think About the Procedure
❶ What will you observe?

_____

❷ Why will you use a hand lens?

_____

_____

_____

Record Your Data

Write and draw to record what you observe.

My Observations	
What I See	
What I Hear	
What I Feel	
What I Smell	

Draw Conclusions

What did you find out about the living things and the habitat?

_____

_____

Ask More Questions

What other questions could you ask about living things?

_____

_____

1.3.1 Classify living organisms according to variations in specific physical features, such as body coverings or appendages, and describe how those features may provide an advantage for survival in different environments.

Lesson 3

Essential Question

What Are Some Kinds of Plants?

Engage Your Brain!

Find the answer to the question in the lesson.

What holds this tree in place?

its _____

Lesson Vocabulary

1 Preview the lesson.

2 Write the 6 vocabulary terms here.

_____   _____

_____   _____

131

A Plant's Makeup

A plant has parts that help it get what it needs to live.

Taking Root

A plant has roots that grow into the soil. The **roots** hold the plant in place. They take in water and other things the plant needs from the soil.

roots

Stems Stand Tall

The **stem** holds up the plant. It takes water from the roots to the other parts of the plant.

A flower has a thin, soft stem. A tree has a thick, woody stem.

stems

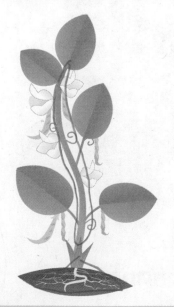

▶ Draw a triangle around the roots of the bean plant. Draw a circle around the stem.

Leaves at Work

A **leaf** is a plant part that makes food for the plant. It uses light, air, and water.

Active Reading

Find the sentence that tells the meaning of **leaf**. Draw a line under the sentence.

Leaves can be different shapes and sizes.

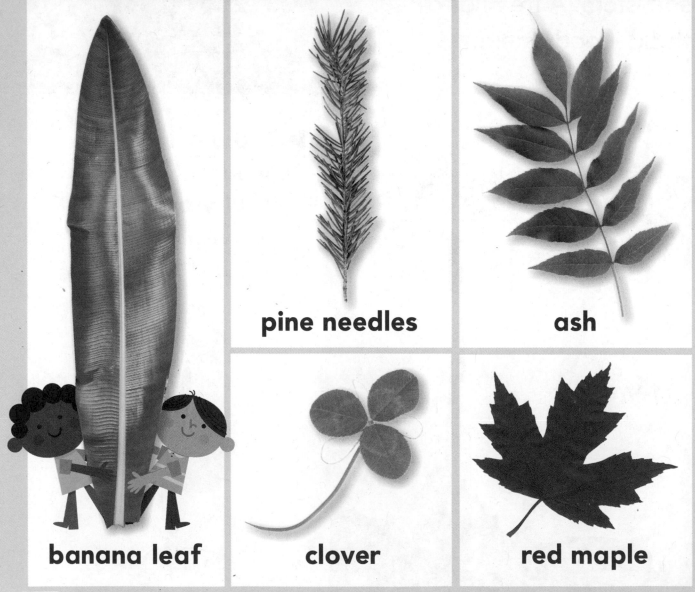

banana leaf

pine needles

clover

ash

red maple

Flowers, Seeds, and Fruit

Many plants have flowers. A **flower** is a plant part that makes seeds. A new plant may grow from a **seed**. The new plant will look like the plant that made the seed.

Many flowers grow into fruits. A **fruit** holds seeds.

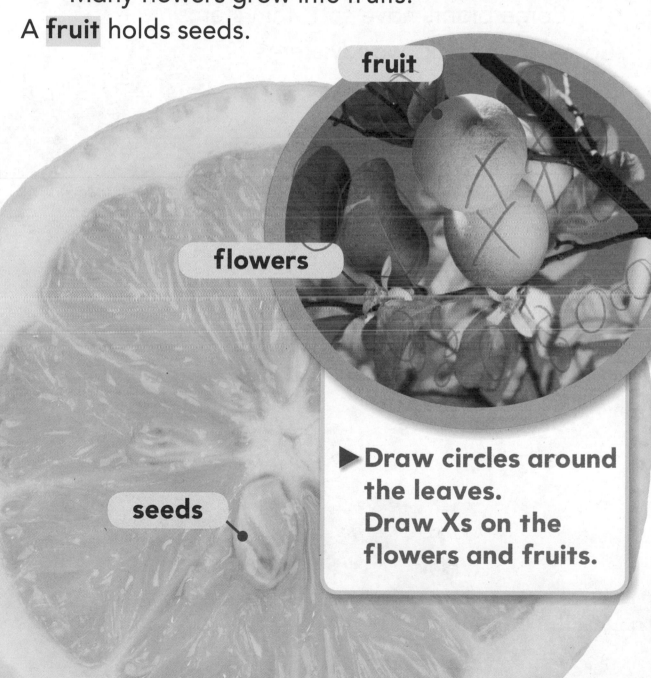

fruit

flowers

seeds

▶ Draw circles around the leaves. Draw Xs on the flowers and fruits.

Plenty of Plants

How can you tell plants apart? They have different leaves and stems. They have different shapes. They can be big or small.

Some plants have soft, thin stems. Some have thick, woody stems.

Trees

- tall
- woody trunk
- many branches
- different leaves
- long life

oak tree

Shrubs

- shorter than trees
- smaller woody stems
- smaller branches
- different leaves
- long life

boxwood shrub

Grasses

- small plants
- soft stems
- long thin leaves
- shorter life

ornamental grasses

▶ Circle the names of the plants with woody stems. Draw a line under the name of the plant with soft stems.

Plants with Flowers

Some plants have flowers. Flowers make a plant's seeds. Flowers can grow on small plants. They can also grow on shrubs and trees. Where have you seen flowers?

hibiscus plant

▶ **What do flowers do?**

Make seeds

Plants with Cones

Some plants have cones. Cones hold a plant's seeds. Cones grow on some trees. Where have you seen cones?

Active Reading

A detail is a fact about a main idea. Draw one line under a detail. Draw an arrow to the main idea it tells about.

pinecone

pine tree

Plant Power

We use plants for food. We also use plants to make things. We use mint leaves in some toothpastes. Flowers make perfume smell good. Woody stems help make our homes. We even use plants to make some medicines. What other plant uses can you name?

Do the Math!
Solve a Problem

Look at the tomatoes. Use them to help you solve this problem.

There are 24 tomatoes.
A farmer picks 11 tomatoes.
How many are left?

24 - 11 = 13

Sum It Up!

① Choose It!

Circle the plant part that takes in water.

② Circle It!

Circle the plant that has cones.

③ Solve It!

Solve the riddle.

I can be thick or thin.
I can be short or tall.
I help a plant get
water and hold it up
so it won't fall.

What am I?

stem

Name _____

Word Play

Label the parts of the plant.

| flower | leaf | roots | stem |

f b wer

leaf

stem

roots

Apply Concepts

Tell which plant parts the plant needs.

Problem	Solution
1 I need a plant part to hold seeds. What part do I need?	cone
2 I need a plant part to take in water. What part do I need?	roots
3 I need a plant part to make fruit. What part do I need?	flower
4 I need a plant part to make food. What part do I need?	leaf
5 I need a plant part to hold me up. What part do I need?	stem
6 I need a plant part to make a new plant. What part do I need?	fruit

© Houghton Mifflin Harcourt Publishing Company

Learn About...
Lue Gim Gong

Lue Gim Gong was born in China. He moved to the United States when he was 12 years old. He spent much of his life in Florida. He did experiments with fruits. His experiments made new fruits. His most famous fruit is called the Lue Gim Gong orange.

Fun Fact

Bees help flowers make new plants.

A Lue Gim Gong Time Line

▶ **Use the time line to answer the questions below.**

Lue Gim Gong is born in China.

In his 20s, he grows the first Lue Gim Gong orange.

He comes to the United States as a boy.

Today farmers still grow Lue Gim Gong oranges.

1. **Where was Lue Gim Gong born? Draw a box around the name of that country.**

2. **How old was Lue Gim Gong when he grew his first Lue Gim Gong orange? Draw a triangle around the words that tell you.**

3. **What do farmers do today? Draw a line under the words that tell you.**

Lesson 4

Essential Question

How Are Animals Different?

 **Engage Your Brain!**

Find the answer to the question in the lesson.

This animal is not an insect. What is it?

_____

Active Reading

Lesson Vocabulary

1. Preview the lesson.

2. Write the 6 vocabulary terms here.

_____   _____

_____   _____

All Kinds of Animals

Animals have different shapes and sizes. They have body parts that help them move in different ways. Some animals walk and run. Others fly or swim.

Animals have different body coverings. Some have fur or hair. Others have scales or feathers.

Active Reading

Clue words can help you find ways things are different. **Different** is a clue word. Draw a box around this word.

Ways to Group Animals

feathers

scarlet macaw

fur

spider monkey

swim

river dolphin

climb

red-eyed tree frog

big

capybara

small

leaf-cutter ants

▶ Circle the words that help group animals by the way they move.

golden lion tamarin

giant anteater

Mammals

A **mammal** has fur or hair. Most mammals have live young. A young mammal drinks milk from its mother's body. People are mammals.

▶ Label the body covering you see.

fur

jaguar

quetzal

toucan

Birds

A **bird** has feathers. Birds also have a beak and wings. Most birds use wings to fly. Birds lay eggs. They find food to feed their young.

parrot

▶ Label the body covering you see.

feathers

151

Reptiles

A **reptile** has dry skin. It is covered in scales. Most reptiles lay eggs. Most reptiles have four legs. But snakes are reptiles with no legs. Turtles are reptiles. They may have legs or flippers. A turtle also has a shell on its back.

green iguanas

caiman

▶ **Label the body covering you see.**

scales

Amphibians

Most **amphibians** have smooth, wet skin. Toads are amphibians with rough, bumpy skin.

Amphibians lay their eggs in water. Young amphibians live in the water. Most grown amphibians live on land.

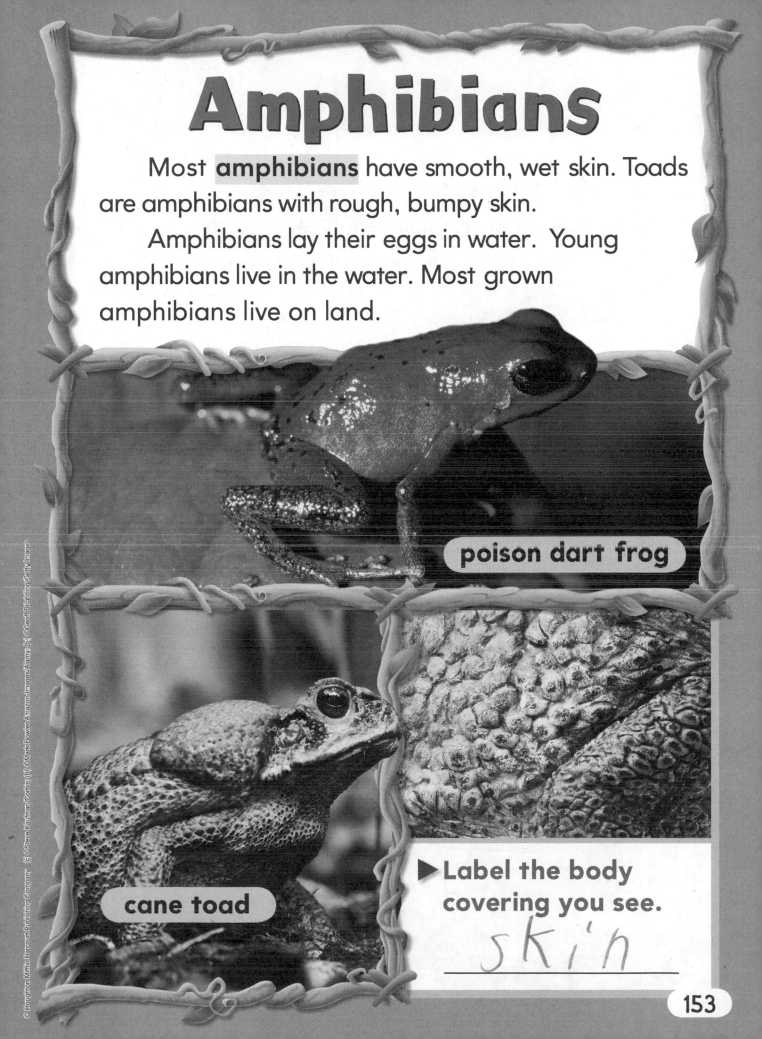

poison dart frog

cane toad

▶ Label the body covering you see.

skin

Fish

Fish have body parts that help them live in water. Most **fish** have scales. The scales help keep their bodies safe. Fish have fins to swim. They have gills to take in oxygen.

Active Reading

The main idea is the most important idea about something. Draw two lines under the main idea.

red piranha

silver dollar fish

▶ **Label the body covering you see.**

scales

Name _____

Word Play

Unscramble the letters to name six animal groups.

| reptile | mammal | fish | amphibian | insect | bird |

lammam   m (a) m m a l

esctni   i (n) s e c t

drib   b (i) r d

phibiaman   ◯ _ _ _ _ _ _ ◯ _

plitree   _ _ _ _ ◯ _

isfh   _ _ ◯ _

Write the circled letters in order to complete the sentence.

There are many different kinds

of _____ .

Apply Concepts

Draw or write an animal from each group.

Animal Groups

Animal Group	Animal from That Group
❶ mammal	
❷ bird	
❸ reptile	
❹ amphibian	
❺ fish	
❻ insect	

Take It Home!

Family Members: Discuss animal groups with your child. Look through magazines and help your child group the animals you see.

Multiple Choice

Fill in the circle next to the best answer.

1.3.2

1 Which shows animals in the place they live?

○

○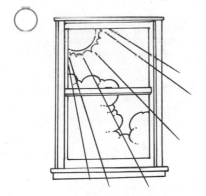

○

1.3.1

2 You see a living thing that can move on its own. What is it?

○ an animal

○ a shrub

○ a tree

1.3.1

3 Which young animals drink milk from their mothers' bodies?

○ birds

○ mammals

○ reptiles

1.3.1

❹ **What plant parts does Number 3 show?**

- ○ flowers
- ○ leaves
- ○ roots

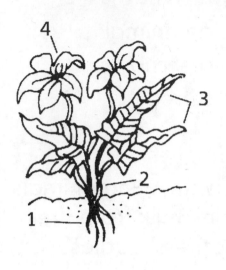

1.3.1, 1.3.3

❺ **What is TRUE about this dog?**

- ○ It makes its own food.
- ○ It is covered with fur.
- ○ It does not need to take in water.

1.3.3

6 Which is TRUE about living things?

○ Living things grow, change, and reproduce.

○ Living things do not grow, change, and reproduce.

○ Living things do not get rid of waste.

1.3.1

7 What kind of animal does this picture show?

○ birds
○ insects
○ mammals

1.3.3

8 How are plants DIFFERENT from animals?

○ Plants make their own food.

○ Plants have to get rid of waste.

○ Plants move around on their own.

1.3.3

9 How do animals get their food?

○ They eat plants, other animals, or both.

○ They make their own food.

○ Animals do not eat food.

Review and ISTEP+ Practice **Unit 4** 161

Use this picture to answer questions 10 and 11.

1.3.2, 1.3.3

⑩ **Which is a living thing in this picture?**
- ○ the rocks
- ○ the shark
- ○ the water

1.3.2, 1.3.3

⑪ **What is TRUE about the fish?**
- ○ They make seeds.
- ○ They make their own food.
- ○ They move around on their own.

1.3.1

⑫ **How are an apple and a pinecone ALIKE?**
- ○ They are both fruits.
- ○ They both hold seeds.
- ○ They grow on the same kind of tree.

1.3.2

⑬ **What can you learn by observing a squirrel in a lawn or a tree?**
- ○ how old it is
- ○ what it eats
- ○ where it was born

1.3.2

⑭ **You observe living things in a terrarium. How can you record your observations?**
- ○ talk about them
- ○ think about them
- ○ write or draw them

1.3.1

15 Which is TRUE about all these animals?

- ◯ They have fur or hair.
- ◯ They are the same size.
- ◯ They have scales.

1.3.1

16 Which is TRUE about all fish?

- ◯ Fish do not need to take in oxygen.
- ◯ Fish use gills to take in oxygen.
- ◯ Fish use lungs to take in oxygen.

1.3.1

17 How do you know that this animal is a bird?

- ◯ It has a beak, feathers, and wings.
- ◯ It drinks milk from its mother's body.
- ◯ It has two eyes.

1.3.1

18 Which animal does NOT lay eggs?

- ◯ a duck
- ◯ an elephant
- ◯ a frog

Use this picture to answer questions 19 and 20.

1.3.1

19 What kind of animal does this picture show?

○ a bird

○ a fish

○ an insect

1.3.1

20 How do you know what kind of animal it is?

○ It has four legs and fur.

○ It has three body parts and six legs.

○ It has a beak, feathers, and wings.

Plant and Animal Needs

Indianapolis Zoo,
Indianapolis, Indiana

I Wonder Why

A vet is feeding this baby giraffe. Why?
Turn the page to find out.

INDIANAPOLIS ZOO

Here's Why In zoos, vets and zoo keepers make sure the animals get what they need to live and grow.

Track Your Progress

Essential Questions and Indiana Standards

STANDARD 3
Life Science

Observe, describe and ask questions about living things and their relationship to their environment.

1.3.3. Observe and explain that plants and animals have basic needs for growth and survival: plants need to take in water and need light and animals need to take in water and food and have a way to dispose of waste.

Essential Question

What Do Plants Need?

Engage Your Brain!

Find the answer to the question in the lesson.

How does this plant grow without soil?

Its roots take in

_____

_____ .

Active Reading

Lesson Vocabulary

1 Preview the lesson.

2 Write the 2 vocabulary terms here.

_____   _____

Plant Needs

Sunlight, Air, and Water

A plant needs certain things to live and grow. A plant needs **sunlight**, or light from the sun. It needs air and water. A plant uses these things to make its food.

As a plant makes food, it needs to give off gases as waste. The gases come out of tiny holes in the leaves.

Active Reading

The main idea is the most important idea about something. Draw two lines under the main idea.

Air is all around, even though we can not see it.

Plants grow toward the sun to get the sunlight they need.

Plants get most of the water they need from the soil.

▶ **Circle three words that name things a plant needs.**

From the Soil

Most plants need soil to grow. **Soil** is made up of small pieces of rock and once-living things. A plant's roots take in water from the soil.

Not all plants grow in soil. Some plants live and grow on other plants. Their roots take in rain and water from the air.

Active Reading

A detail is a fact about a main idea. Draw one line under a detail. Draw an arrow to the main idea it tells about.

Space to Grow

As a plant grows, its stem gets taller. Its roots get bigger. It grows more leaves, too. A plant must have enough space to grow.

▶ **What does this farmer do to make sure his crop grows?**

space

good soil

People Helping Plants

How do people help plants? They water plants. They pull weeds so plants have space to grow. People put plants by windows so plants can get sunlight.

Active Reading

Clue words can help you find an effect. **So** is a clue word. Draw a box around **so**.

People also help plants by planting new ones. They plant seeds so new flowers can grow. They plant young trees so people can enjoy them.

▶**How do you help plants?**

Pat corn protet the plants!

Sum It Up!

① Circle It!

Circle two things that a plant needs.

② Write It!

This plant has gotten too big for its pot.

What need is not being met?

_____

Name _____

Word Play

Color in the words that name things a plant needs.

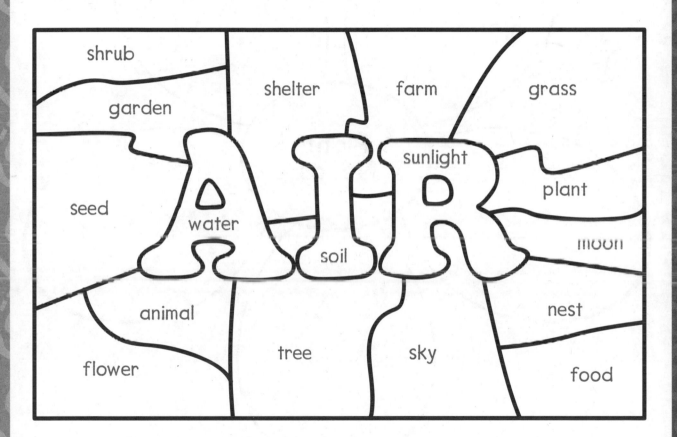

Now answer the question.

What is all around us?

_____

Complete the web to tell what plants need to grow and be healthy.

Plant Needs

1.3.3 Observe and explain that plants and animals have basic needs for growth and survival; plants need to take in water and need light and animals need to take in water and food and have a way to dispose of waste.

Name _____

Essential Question

Why Do Plants Grow?

Set a Purpose
Tell what you want to find out.

_____

_____

Think About the Procedure
❶ What will you observe?

_____

_____

❷ How will you treat the plants differently?

_____

_____

Record Your Data

In this chart, record what you observe.

My Observations of Two Plants		
	Plant A	**Plant B**
How the stems look		
How the leaves look		
Other observations		

Draw Conclusions

Can a plant grow when it does not get what it needs?

_____

_____

Ask More Questions

What other questions could you ask about plant needs?

_____

_____

Oxygen

Animals need **oxygen**, a gas in air. Land animals use their lungs to breathe in oxygen. Some water animals, such as whales, have lungs. They breathe air. Fish do not have lungs. They use **gills** to get oxygen.

A black bear eats berries.

gills

A fish uses gills to take in oxygen from the water.

▶ **Which animal uses its gills to get oxygen?**

_____

Shelter

Most animals need shelter. A **shelter** is a place where an animal can be safe. An animal may use a plant as a shelter. It may dig a hole in the ground. It may even use another animal as a shelter. One animal that does this is a clownfish.

Kinds of Animal Shelters

A prairie dog lives in a burrow.

A beaver lives in a lodge.

Some birds lay eggs in a nest.

A skunk lives in a den.

▶ Draw an animal in its shelter.

Space

Animals need space to grow. They need space to move around and find food.

Animals need space for shelter. They need space to take care of their young.

Active Reading

A detail is a fact about a main idea. Draw one line under a detail. Draw an arrow to the main idea it tells about.

A cheetah needs space to run and catch its food.

Your Needs

You are a living thing. You must meet your needs to grow and stay healthy. What do you and other people need? You need oxygen to breathe. You need food and water. You need space and shelter.

► **How are the needs of people like the needs of animals?**

_____

_____

Caring for Pets

Pets are animals. Think about some pets you know. Where do they get their food and water? Who gives them shelter? They need people to help them meet their needs.

Taking care of a pet is a big job. A pet needs space to exercise and play. You need to keep the pet and its shelter clean. You must clean up after a pet, too.

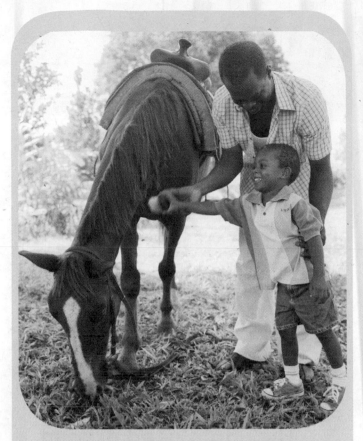

People need to take care of pets and keep them clean.

People need to give pets food.

This dog gets 1 cup of dog food in the morning and 1 cup of dog food at night.

How many cups of dog food does it get for one day?

1 cup in morning

+ 1 cup at night

____

____ cups in one day

How many cups of dog food does it get for five days?

_____

Sum It Up!

① Choose It!

Mark an X on the one that does <u>not</u> belong.

Animal Needs

water   sunlight

oxygen   food

getting rid of waste

② Circle It!

How are people and animals alike?

They both need soil.

They both live in dens.

They both need sunlight.

They both need oxygen and water.

③ Draw It!

Draw an animal meeting each need.

Food	Water

Name _____

Word Play

Pets need things to help them live and grow.
Fill in the words to tell what a hamster needs.

oxygen   food   shelter   space to grow   water

o_____

w_____

s_____

s_____   f_____

Apply Concepts

Think about how you meet your needs each day. Then fill in the chart below.

You Need	How You Meet Your Needs
1 oxygen	_____ _____
2 _____	I drink from the water fountain at soccer practice.
3 food	_____ _____
4 _____	I go inside my house when it rains.
5 space to grow	_____ _____

Take It Home!

Family Members: Discuss with your child what animals and people need to grow and stay healthy. Ask your child to tell you how his or her needs are met.

Essential Question

How Do Plants and Animals Need One Another?

Engage Your Brain!

Find the answer to the question in the lesson.

This bat drinks from the plant. How is the bat also helping the plant?

The bat spreads *pollen* .

Active Reading

Lesson Vocabulary

❶ Preview the lesson.

❷ Write the vocabulary term here.

_____

Getting Help

Animals use plants to meet their needs. Many animals use plants for shelter. Some animals hide in plants. Other animals live in plants or use them to build homes.

Active Reading

A detail is a fact about a main idea. Draw one line under a detail. Draw an arrow to the main idea it tells about.

An owl finds shelter in a tree.

A lion hides in tall grass.

Some animals spread pollen for plants. **Pollen** is a powder that flowers need to make seeds. Pollen may stick to an animal. The animal carries the pollen from flower to flower. This helps plants make new plants.

As a bat drinks the flower nectar, pollen rubs off on the bat.

A beetle carries pollen on its body.

A woodpecker moves seeds with its beak.

▶ Underline two ways animals help plants.

1 Circle It!

Circle the pictures of animals helping plants.

2 Label It!

Write <u>food</u> or <u>shelter</u> to tell how each animal is using plants.

shelter

shelter

food

food shelter

Name _____

Word Play

Draw the path from each word to its meaning.

Apply Concepts

Use words from the word bank to complete the chart.

shelter	oxygen	seeds	food	pollen

Ways Animals Use Plants	Ways Animals Help Plants
When animals build nests, they use plants for ___shelter___.	Animals carry ___seeds___ to new places.
Animals eat plants as ___food___.	Animals spread ___pollen___ that sticks to their bodies.
Animals breathe ___oxygen___ that plants give off. oxygen	

Take It Home!

Family Members: Take a walk outside with your child. Help your child observe animals using plants.

198

1.3.1 Classify living organisms according to variations in specific physical features, such as body coverings or appendages, and describe how those features may provide an advantage for survival in different environments. **1.3.4** Describe how animals' habitats, including plants, meet their needs for food, water, shelter, and an environment in which they can live.

Lesson **5**

Essential Question

Where Do Plants and Animals Live?

🧠 Engage Your Brain!

Find the answer to the question in the lesson.

What animal might live in this environment?

_____

_____

Active Reading

Lesson Vocabulary

1 Preview the lesson.

2 Write the 2 vocabulary terms here.

_____   _____

All Around You

Look around. All the living and nonliving things you see make up your **environment**. A living thing lives in the environment that meets its needs.

A **habitat** is a smaller part of an environment. A habitat is the place where a living thing gets food, water, and shelter.

Active Reading

Circle the words that tell what a **habitat** is.

Some foxes live in a forest environment.

Salty Water

An ocean environment is a large body of salt water. Its top layer is home to many living things. Here, plants get sunlight. Animals find food.

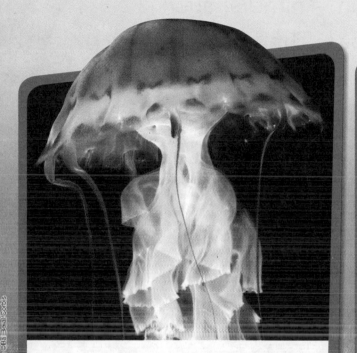

A jellyfish has body parts that help it catch its food.

Kelp lives in the ocean. Many animals eat it.

► **Why do many plants live in the top layer of the ocean?**

because there is the most sun

In a Rain Forest

A rain forest gets a lot of rain. The trees grow tall and block the sun. Animals, such as birds, live in the tall trees. The plants below do not need much sunlight.

These living things can live in the rain forest because it meets their needs.

▶ Draw a rain forest animal that might live in the trees.

Dry As a Bone

A desert environment gets little rain. Plants store water in their thick stems or leaves. In hot deserts, many animals hide during the day.

A Joshua tree can be a habitat for small animals.

Desert plants and animals can live with little water.

desert hare

Gila monster

▶Draw a cactus.

cactus

It's Cold Out Here!

A tundra is a very cold environment.
Plants grow close together near the ground.
Animals have thick fur to stay warm.

An Arctic fox's white fur helps it hide in the snow.

▶ **How does an Arctic fox's white fur help it in winter?**

_____

_____

_____

purple saxifrage flowers

On the Prairie

A prairie environment is mostly dry. It has just a few kinds of trees and shrubs. Large animals eat the tall grasses. Smaller animals live in the grasses.

Active Reading

Read the labels. Circle the name of the small animal that lives in prairie grasses.

Bison travel in herds eating prairie grasses.

coneflowers

prairie dogs

red-tailed hawk

Sum It Up!

① Draw It!

Choose an environment. Draw a living thing meeting its needs there.

② Label It!

Name the environment in which you would find each living thing.

_____   _____   _____

Name _____

Word Play

Use the words below to complete the puzzle.

habitat   ~~desert~~   ~~environment~~
~~prairie~~   tundra   ~~rain forest~~

Across

1. a very cold environment

2. a dry, grassy environment

3. a very dry environment

Down

4. all living and nonliving things in a place

5. an environment with a lot of rain

6. a place where a living thing meets its needs

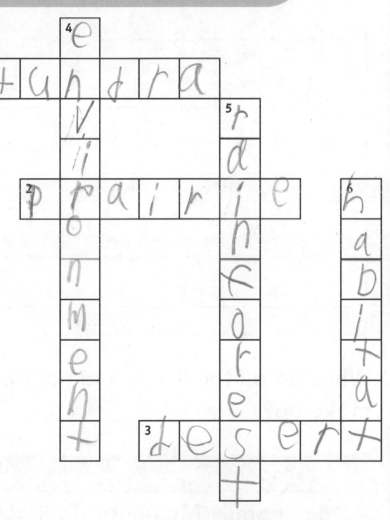

Crossword puzzle answers:
1 Across: tundra
2 Across: prairie
3 Across: desert
4 Down: environment
5 Down: rain forest
6 Down: habitat

Apply Concepts

Write two details that go with the main idea. Then answer the question.

Main Idea
A tundra is a cold environment.

Detail–Animals	Detail–Plants
_____	_____
_____	_____
_____	_____
_____	_____
_____	_____

What do all the living and nonliving things in a place make up? _____

© Houghton Mifflin Harcourt Publishing Company

1.3.3 Observe and explain that plants and animals have basic needs for growth and survival. . .
1.3.4 Describe how animals' habitats, including plants, meet their needs for food, water, shelter, and an environment in which they can live.

Careers in Science

Ask a Zoo Keeper

What does a zoo keeper do?

I feed the animals. I give them water. I make sure that the animals are healthy. I also keep their environments clean.

How do you know when an animal is sick?

Animals can not tell me when they don't feel well. So I observe them carefully. Sometimes an animal eats or moves very little. That could be a sign that the animal is sick.

What else does a zoo keeper do?

I talk to people about the zoo animals. I have fun talking to children. They like animals so much!

Now It's Your Turn!

▶ **What question would you ask a zoo keeper?**

_____

_____

Now You Be a Zoo Keeper!

▶ **A tiger cub was born at your zoo. Make a plan to take care of the cub.**

My Zoo Keeper Plan

 I will _____ _____ .

 I will _____ _____ .

 I will _____ _____ .

Essential Question

How Are Animal Shelters Alike and Different?

Engage Your Brain!

Find the answer to the question in the lesson.

Hornets use a nest to meet what need?

_____

Active Reading

Lesson Vocabulary

❶ Preview the lesson.

❷ Write the vocabulary term here.

_____

Safe and Snug

Animals need shelters. Shelters keep animals and their young safe. Some animals find shelters. Others build shelters.

Active Reading

Draw a line under the sentence that tells the meaning of **tool**.

A robin builds a nest to keep its chicks safe.

A fox stays safe and dry under a rock.

A mole digs a burrow to be safe and find food.

Animal Builders

Animals use different materials and tools to build shelters. They find materials in their habitats.

Animals use body parts as tools. A **tool** is something that helps do work. Beaks, teeth, and paws are tools for some animals.

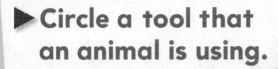
► Circle a tool that an animal is using.

A weaverbird uses its beak to weave grasses into a nest.

A beaver uses its teeth and paws to build its lodge from trees.

Not All the Same

Shelters are not all the same. Look at this termite mound. It is tall. It rests on top of the ground. Termites build the mound with soil. Inside, tunnels join the rooms.

Active Reading

When you contrast things, you find out ways they are different. Draw triangles around two things that are being contrasted.

termite mound

A termite mound has rooms and tunnels inside.

A prairie dog burrow has rooms and tunnels, too. Prairie dogs use their paws to dig in soil. They make rooms and tunnels below ground.

prairie dog in a burrow

A prairie dog burrow has tunnels below ground.

▶ How is a prairie dog burrow different from a termite mound?

The burrow is

_____.

Sum It Up!

① Match It!

Draw a line from each shelter to its name.

nest   burrow   lodge

② Circle It!

Circle the shelters built by animals. The first one is done for you.

Name _____

Word Play

Look across and down to find four words you know. Circle them.

p	s	x	m	o	n	s
s	h	v	k	j	z	e
f	e	b	l	u	s	b
n	l	s	a	s	t	u
c	t	o	o	l	d	i
t	e	e	t	h	q	l
y	r	h	a	r	g	d

Use the words from the puzzle to complete the sentences.

1 A _____ helps a person or animal do work.

2 Animals need _____ to keep safe.

3 Termites _____ mounds above the ground.

4 Some animals use their _____ to build.

Apply Concepts

Fill in the diagram to compare the shelters.
Use words from the box.

soil	trees	paws	safe	ground	water

Beaver Lodge

- built from

_____

- in

_____

Both

- keep animals

_____

- built by
  animals using

_____

Prairie Dog Burrow

- built in

_____

- under the

_____

Take It Home!

Family Members: Observe the shelters of animals near your home. Talk with your child about how the shelters are alike and how they are different.

© Houghton Mifflin Harcourt Publishing Company

218

Multiple Choice
Fill in the circle next to the best answer.

1.3.3

❶ What do both of these living things need to live?

- ○ rocks
- ○ soil
- ○ water

1.4.2

❷ What kind of shelter does this animal live in?

- ○
- ○
- ○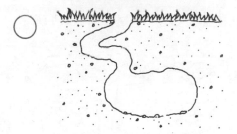

1.3.3

❸ Which is a reason that plants need sunlight?

- ○ to make water
- ○ to make their food
- ○ to have space to grow

1.3.3

4 Which part of the plant takes in water from the soil?

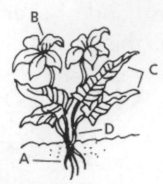

○ part A
○ part B
○ part C

1.3.3

5 You set up two plants this way. What question could you investigate?

○ Do plants need water to live?
○ Do plants need light to live?
○ Do plants need warm air to live?

1.3.3

6 You set up an investigation with four plants of the same kind.

Plant 1 gets light and water.

Plant 2 gets light but no water.

Plant 3 gets water but no light.

Plant 4 gets no water and no light.

Plant 1 grows well. The other plants die. What can you conclude?

○ Plants need only water to live.
○ Plants need only light to live.
○ Plants need both light and water to live.

1.3.3

7 A plant needs more space to grow. Which do you predict would give it more space?

- ○ giving it more water
- ○ putting more plants around it
- ○ pulling up weeds around it

1.3.4

8 In which environment does this bird get what it needs to live?

- ○ a desert
- ○ a prairie
- ○ a rain forest

Use this picture to answer questions 9 and 10.

1.3.5

9 How is the bird using the tree?

- ○ as food
- ○ as shelter
- ○ for water

1.3.5

10 How is the deer using the leaves of the tree?

- ○ as food
- ○ as shelter
- ○ for space

1.3.5

11 A bee carries pollen from flower to flower. What is it doing?

○ using the flowers for shelter

○ giving the flowers more space to grow

○ helping plants make new plants

1.3.4

12 Which is a smaller part of an environment where a living thing gets what it needs to live?

○ a habitat

○ a prairie

○ a shelter

1.3.1

13 Why do desert plants have thick stems or leaves for storing water?

○ A desert is very wet.

○ A desert gets only a little rain.

○ A desert has only a few animals.

1.3.1

14 This animal lives in the tundra. How does its white fur help the animal stay alive?

○ It helps the animal hide in the snow.

○ It keeps the animal cool in summer.

○ It helps the animal store water.

1.3.4

15 Which is TRUE?

○ All animals live in a rain forest.

○ Animals that live in a desert can also live in a tundra.

○ Animals live in an environment that meets their needs.

1.4.2

16 How are these shelters the SAME?

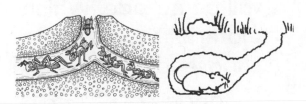

○ The same animal uses them.

○ They are both tunnels underground.

○ They are both made from leaves and twigs.

1.4.2

17 What tools do some animals use to build their shelters?

○ hammer and nails

○ their eyes and ears

○ their beaks, teeth, or paws

1.4.2

18 Two animals are building shelters. What is ALIKE?

○ Both animals are digging under the ground.

○ Both animals are using trees.

○ Both animals are making nests.

Use this information to answer questions 19 and 20.

Tyler is getting a pet rabbit. He has to keep it outside.

1.4.3

19 How can Tyler keep the rabbit safe?

○ build a shelter for it

○ give it water

○ play with it

1.4.3

20 Tyler will make a rabbit shelter. The shelter will be outside. Which material should he choose for the shelter?

○ fabric

○ paper

○ wood

UNIT 6
Engineering and Materials

PROCESS STANDARDS
Design Process

Butterfly Meadows, Valparaiso, Indiana

I Wonder How
An engineer planned a design for this playground. How?
Turn the page to find out.

Here's How An engineer drew ideas on a plan. The plan had many fun things for kids.

Track Your Progress

Essential Questions and Indiana Standards

PROCESS STANDARDS
Design Process

As citizens of the constructed world, students will participate in the design process. Students will learn to use materials and tools safely and employ the basic principles of the engineering design process in order to find solutions to problems.

The Design Process As citizens of the constructed world, students will participate in the design process. Students will learn to use materials and tools safely and employ the basic principles of the engineering design process in order to find solutions to problems.

Essential Question

How Do Engineers Work?

Engage Your Brain!

Find the answer to the question in the lesson.

How do you scratch an itch you can not reach?

You can

_____

_____ .

Active Reading

Lesson Vocabulary

1 Preview the lesson.

2 Write the 2 vocabulary terms here.

_____ _____

Problem Solvers

An **engineer** uses math and science to solve everyday problems. Engineers work on many kinds of problems. Some engineers design robots. Others plan roads. Some design cars.

Active Reading

A detail is a fact about a main idea. Draw one line under a detail about **engineers**. Draw an arrow to the main idea it tells about.

▶ **Circle the names of three kinds of engineers.**

robotics engineer

Engineers use a design process to solve problems. A **design process** is a plan with steps that help engineers find good solutions.

The Design Process

1. Find a problem. Brainstorm ideas.
2. Keep good records.
3. Plan a solution. Choose materials.
4. Build the solution.
5. Test the solution.
6. Communicate the results.

mechanical engineer

civil engineer

The Design Process

1 Find a problem. Brainstorm ideas.

Jack has an itch he can not reach. How can he scratch it? The steps of this design process show Jack what to do.

Jack names his problem. He needs to find a way to scratch his back. He brainstorms ways to solve his problem.

Jack tries to scratch his back.

▶ **What problem does Jack want to solve?**

Jack wants to find away to scratch his back

Jack shows what happened in his test. He draws and labels his back scratcher. He adds notes about how to make it better.

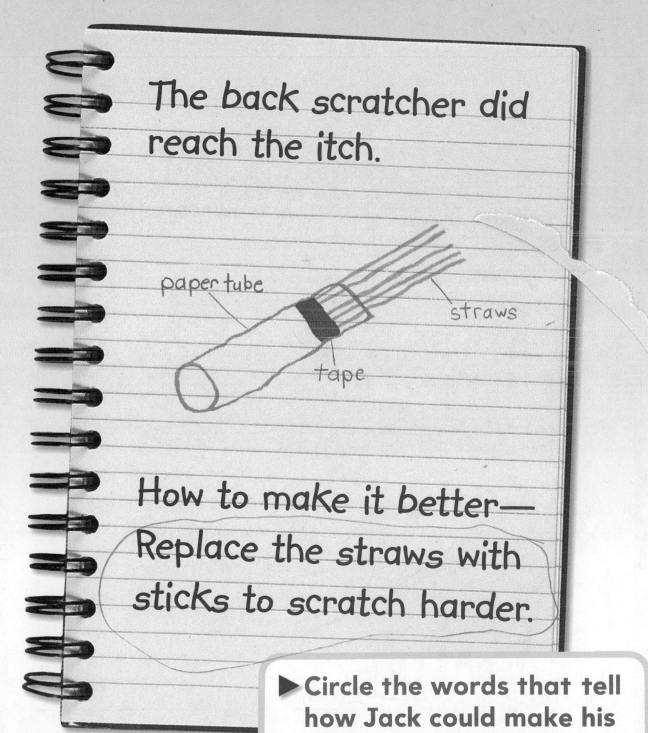

The back scratcher did reach the itch.

paper tube

straws

tape

How to make it better— Replace the straws with sticks to scratch harder.

▶ Circle the words that tell how Jack could make his back scratcher better.

Sum It Up!

① Circle It!

Circle the step of the design process shown in the picture.

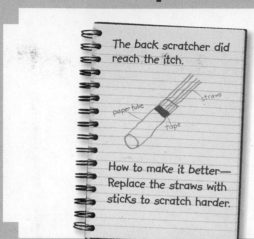

The back scratcher did reach the itch.

paper tube straws tape

How to make it better— Replace the straws with sticks to scratch harder.

Build the solution.

Test the solution.

Communicate the results.

② Solve It!

Answer the riddle.

I solve problems using science and math. The design process leads me along the right path. Who am I?

an engineer

Word Play

Write a label for each picture.

choose materials   build   engineer   test

choose materiis

test

build

engineer

Apply Concepts

Write the numbers 1 to 6 to order the steps of the design process. The first one is done for you.

The Design Process

___3___ Plan a solution. Choose materials.

___1___ Find a problem. Brainstorm ideas.

___5___ Test the solution.

___6___ Communicate the results.

___4___ Build the solution.

___2___ Keep good records.

The Design Process As citizens of the constructed world, students will participate in the design process. Students will learn to use materials and tools safely and employ the basic principles of the engineering design process in order to find solutions to problems.

Name _____

Essential Question

How Can We Solve a Problem?

Set a Purpose
Tell what you will do.

_____

_____

Think About the Procedure

1 What steps will you follow to build your stand?

_____

_____

_____

2 How will you know that your stand works?

_____

Record Your Data

Draw the plan for your solution.

Draw Conclusions

Draw and label a picture that shows what happened.

How did your solution work? What would you change?

_____

_____

Ask More Questions

What other questions could you ask about designing a
solution to a problem?

_____

_____

The Design Process As citizens of the constructed world, students will participate in the design process. Students will learn to use materials and tools safely and employ the basic principles of the engineering design process in order to find solutions to problems.

People in Science

Get to Know Dr. Eugene Tsui

Dr. Eugene Tsui is an architect. This is a kind of engineer. An architect designs homes and other buildings.

Dr. Tsui studies forms in nature, such as sea shells. He bases his designs on what he learns. Dr. Tsui says that nature is our great teacher.

Fun Fact

Dr. Tsui also designs his own clothes.

241

Dr. Tsui's Designs

▶ Draw a line from each building to the natural form it is based on.

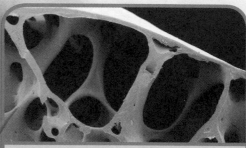
the bones of a bird

fish scales

dragonfly wings

▶ Think about a form from nature. Use it to design your own building.

Multiple Choice

Fill in the circle next to the best answer.

Design Process

1 What do engineers use to solve everyday problems?

○ history and math

○ math and science

○ music and art

Design Process

2 What kind of work do engineers do?

○ All engineers build roads.

○ All engineers design cars.

○ All engineers solve problems.

Design Process

3 What is the design process?

○ steps that engineers use to solve problems

○ steps that tell how to make a robot

○ steps that tell how to become an engineer

Design Process

4 What is the last step of the design process?

○ Test the solution.

○ Find a problem.

○ Communicate the results.

Use this information to answer questions 5–7.

A river is between two towns. People want to drive from one town to the other. The only way to cross the river is by boat.

Design Process

5 What is the problem?

○ The people are afraid of boats.

○ The people do not have cars.

○ The people do not have a way to get across the river by car.

Design Process

6 Two engineers talk about the problem. How do they plan to solve it?

○ build a tunnel under the river

○ build a bridge over the river

○ give boats to the people in the towns

Design Process

7 Which process can the engineers use to solve their problem?

○ the bridge process
○ the car process
○ the design process

Design Process

8 What is the FIRST step of the design process?

○ Find a problem.
○ Plan a solution.
○ Test the solution.

Design Process

9 You chose these objects to make a solution. Which step of the design process have you done?

○ Build a solution.
○ Choose materials.
○ Find a problem.

Design Process

10 How do you know whether your solution works?

○ ask other people
○ plan the solution
○ test the solution

Design Process

11 You choose materials. Which step is NEXT in the design process?

- ○ Communicate the results.
- ○ Build the solution.
- ○ Test the solution.

Design Process

12 When should you test your solution?

- ○ after you build your solution
- ○ before you choose your materials
- ○ before you plan your solution

Design Process

13 What should you do AFTER you test the solution?

- ○ Choose materials.
- ○ Keep good records.
- ○ Communicate the results.

Use this information to answer questions 14–17.

Ralph's mom has trouble finding her keys. Ralph wants to find a solution for his mom.

Design Process

14 What problem does Ralph want to solve?

○ His mom loses her keys a lot.

○ His mom does not have any keys.

○ His mom does not drive him anywhere.

Design Process

15 Ralph gets wood, hooks, and paint to make a key holder for his mom. Which step of the design process is this?

○ Choose materials.

○ Find a problem.

○ Keep good records.

Design Process

16 Ralph plans his solution. What should be his next step?

○ Test the solution.

○ Communicate the results.

○ Build the solution.

Design Process

17 Ralph makes his solution. Then his mom tries it for a week. Which step does Ralph's mom do?

○ Find a problem.

○ Test the solution.

○ Choose the materials.

Design Process

18 When should you build your solution?

○ before you find a problem

○ after you plan a solution

○ after you communicate your results

Use this information to answer questions 19 and 20.

Lexie needs a place to put her toys. She decides to make a toy box.

Design Process

19 Lexie chooses her materials. Then she makes her toy box. What should she do next?

○ test the box

○ communicate the results of the test

○ find a problem

Design Process

20 Lexie tests the toy box. She finds that the box is not strong enough to hold her toys. What should she do with the results of the test?

○ throw them away and find a new problem to solve

○ use them to test all her toys

○ use them to make a better design for a toy box

F

engineer

Someone who uses math and science to solve problems. (p. 228)

fish

The group of animals that live in water and get oxygen through gills. Fish have scales and use fins to swim. (p. 154)

environment

All the living and nonliving things in a place. (p. 200)

flower

The plant part that makes seeds. (p. 134)

Interactive Glossary

fruit

The part of the plant that holds seeds. (p. 134)

Your Turn

G

gas

A state of matter that fills all the space of its container. (p. 71)

gills

gills

The parts of a fish that take in oxygen from the water. (p. 181)

H

habitat
The place where a living thing finds food, water, and shelter. (p. 200)

human-made
Materials made by people. (p. 54)

Your Turn

I

inquiry skills
Skills that help you find out information. (p. 18)

Falling Leaves Forest

compare

observe

insect
A kind of animal that has three body parts and six legs. (p. 155)

Interactive Glossary

investigation
A test that scientists do. (p. 30)

liquid
A state of matter that flows and takes the shape of its container. (p. 70)

Your Turn

L

leaf
The part of a plant that makes food for the plant. A leaf uses light, air, and water to make food. (p. 133)

living things
Things that are living. People, animals, and plants are living things because they need food, water, air, and space to live. They grow, change, and reproduce. (p. 122)

M

mammal

The group of animals with fur or hair on their bodies. (p. 150)

Your Turn

mass

The amount of matter in an object. (p. 68)

material

What an object is made of. (p. 52)

Interactive Glossary

matter
Anything that takes up space. (p. 68)

oxygen
A gas in the air and water. Most living things need oxygen. (p. 181)

N

natural
Materials found in nature. (p. 54)

Your Turn

P

pollen
A powder that flowers need to make seeds. Some small animals help carry pollen from one flower to another. (p. 195)

property

One part of what something is like. (p. 94)

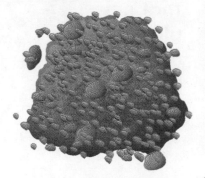

reptile

The group of animals with dry skin covered in scales. (p. 152)

Your Turn

R

reproduce

To make new living things like themselves. (p. 123)

root

The part of a plant that holds the plant in place. The roots take in water. (p. 132)

Interactive Glossary

S

sand
Large bits of rock. It does not hold water well. (p. 93)

science tools
Tools people use to find out about things. (p. 8)

seed
The part of a plant that new plants grow from. (p. 134)

senses
The way you observe and learn. The five senses are sight, hearing, smell, taste, and touch. (p. 4)

Your Turn

shelter

A place where an animal can be safe. (p. 182)

Your Turn

silt

Medium bits of rock. It holds water fairly well. (p. 93)

soil

The top layer of Earth. It is made up of small pieces of rock and once-living things. (pp. 90, 170)

Interactive Glossary

solid
The only state of matter that has its own shape. (p. 70)

Your Turn

sunlight
Light from the sun. (p. 168)

T

tool
Something that helps do work. Animals use body parts as tools. (p. 213)

Your Turn

stem
The part of a plant that holds up the plant. (p. 133)

© Houghton Mifflin Harcourt Publishing Company

Index

Index

Index